Foreword by the Author

Since the Blackpool trams have created my interest from the days of my childhood in Fleetwood, it has not proved too surprising that I have written many books about the local trams! In this book, I have shown highlights from the history, which have not previously been featured. Certainly the Marton trams were distinct from the Promenade, and provided the means of going to Stanley Park - from Talbot Square or South Pier - and were well-liked by the local population and indeed the visitors. When it closed in 1962, Marton had become the last street tram route in Britain, and was sadly missed! Then again, it has been fascinating that Blackpool trams have become popular in the U.S.A., and it was my pleasure to tour San Francisco last year - on Boat 228. It has been fortunate in this book that Roy E. Bonn has contributed the story of Standard 48 operating Willamette Shore Trolley, 37 years since it was here! Of course, the Centenary celebrations in 1998 - of the Blackpool & Fleetwood line - always creates nostalgia for the residents, visitors and the enthusiasts. I hope that you will find this book interesting and also enjoyable. Hold Tight!

Steve Palmer

1928 Pantograph-car 167 briefly seen on Central Promenade with the Tower - for the Centenary in 1998.
Author

Boat-car 228 seen with MUNI 1 on a tour of San Francisco in March 2000, climbing Church Street with a view of the city behind.
Graham Weaver

Marton Trams Around Blackpool – 1901

BOARD OF TRADE INSPECTION

The "Man in the Street" has found some difficulty in digesting the fact that the Marton tram route is really finished, and now the cars are running for his enjoyment. Ever since the new cars made their appearance, they have been the object of much curiosity and speculation. Yesterday morning - 23 May 1901 - there was quite a crowd of spectators in Talbot Square, surveying the cars which were to conduct the Board of Trade Inspectors and their company over the route. The cars to be used on the new line are fifteen in number, and the top deck is fitted with seats having reversible tops and backs, and at night it will be illuminated with a detachable electric globe. There is accommodation for 63 passengers - 39 outside and 24 inside. A preliminary trial trip was made late on Monday night, and again on Tuesday two of the cars were run along the route, bearing members of the Corporation, when everything worked most satisfactorily. In certain localities the public expressed their admiration of the new service by greeting the cars with hearty cheers. The critical and admiring elements were nicely blended in yesterday's crowd, and amongst the busy conversation it was easy to distinguish such comments as: "Didn't think the Corporation were equal to it! Very smart work, but what will the Inspector say about that dangerous step? They are fine cars though, and ought to pay." The conversation gave place to curiosity when Major Druitt - a smart looking young man - made his appearance accompanied by the Town Clerk. In a business-like manner he boarded car 32, which carried flags fore and aft, and made a rapid, but critical inspection of the interior and exterior of the car, bestowing great attention on the position of the step. Round the cars were congregated a number of guards and drivers in all the glory of their new uniforms!

Evening Gazette

Talbot Square and Entrance to North Pier, Blackpool.

A view from Yates's Wine Lodge in 1902, showing the Marton car on the left-hand side of Talbot Square with track now including separate termini for Marton and Layton.

The Board of Trade Inspection

A delightful 1901 view of the new Marton car 40 outside the Oxford Hotel, at the most easterly part of the tramway. A bus can be seen in the background, heading for South Shore.
Barry Shaw

GT. MARTON, BLACKPOOL.

At a quarter to eleven the first car commenced its journey. The second car followed four minutes later, the signal for starting being the appearance of the first car at the top of Clifton Street. The second car maintained a respectable distance, and was brought to a standstill when the first car halted. When car 32 reached the top of Church Street, it was evident to the occupants that something in the form of a demonstration was taking place. Their curiosity was soon satisfied, because the driver found himself confronted with two bicycles fixed securely by the tyres in the half-inch groove of the line. Here a solemn-looking individual held up a large placard containing the words: "Suicide made easy - ride on these tram lines". After everybody on the car had digested the contents of the placard, the bicycles were gravely removed and the journey was continued. So far, the running of the cars had been most smooth and comfortable, the curves and the points were easily negotiated, and the new grooves appeared to answer admirably. In the distance, the first car could be seen to stop now and again, but whether it was because of the trolley becoming detached from the wire, or for the inspection of the line, it was not clear. Opposite Marton Church, it was noted that the crown of the hill had been removed, and the roadway widened. In Central Drive, where the style of rails have been utilised, there was quite a pyrotechnic display as the wheels gripped the rails, and the oscillation was more pronounced. The cars arrived at the Central Station three minutes under the hour, and were then switched over to the other line, in order to make the return journey. As the two cars passed, the Inspector whipped out a two-foot ruler and measured the intervening distance.

Evening Gazette

The second journey was made in a much quicker time, the stops for observation being few and far between. The second car experienced some difficulty with the trolley, which would persist in leaving the wire. Coming down Church Street the electric-brake, which can pull up the car in six feet, was applied. Hand-brakes will allow the car to descend a steep hill slowly and can easily be controlled by the driver. Talbot Square was reached after half-an-hour's run. As the Inspector left the car, he was heard to observe that the step and the lifeguard must be altered, as they were unsatisfactory in their present position. As there was no objection made to the cars running in the afternoon, it may be taken for granted that the permanent way and the general equipment which has cost £100,000 will be satisfactorily passed, and will be put into working order. The line, which is fitted with Mr. Quin's patent "cut-out", guard-wires are placed wherever telephone wires cross the trolley wires. These cars have been built by the firm that built the Promenade Dreadnought cars - the Midland Carriage Works in Shrewsbury - and the electric equipment has been supplied by the British Thompson Houston Company. The trolley standards, arms, pillars and overhead equipment are by Lowdon Bros. of Edinburgh.

Evening Gazette

Talbot Square, for a busy scene in 1901, with the new Marton cars being fully-loaded and carrying a poster in their saloon window. This is before the new line in Clifton Street, and the new Layton route in 1902.

Blackpool Library

Some Problems for the New Marton Tramway

Marton-car 30 on the single-line section, passing the elegant canopy of the Empress Ballroom entrance, and in the foreground St. John's Parish Church fenced grounds.
Vernon Linden

The new route round Marton has made a good commencement, despite the many disadvantages which have so far had to be faced. The receipts for the first five days were about £240, and so it is very evident that the possibilities of the line during the summer are very great indeed. So far, some trouble has been experienced, what with the axles heating, the trolleys being too short, and the gross carelessness of some drivers. However, much delay is caused by the fact that there is no passing-place between Talbot Square and the corner of Church and Abingdon Streets. Frequently during the week, as many as six cars have been waiting in Church Street and Raikes Road, until one comes up from Talbot Square and clears the single line. In the course of time, returning cars will reach Talbot Square by a line which is proposed to be made down Clifton Street. Powers for that line are being sought in the Bill, now at Parliament. We do not see any reason why the Council should not anticipate the result, and have the Clifton Street loop made in June! If that loop is not made before the busy time again, it will certainly mean much delay, inconvenience and loss of fares to the Corporation. Also, it is possible that the Tramway Committee will not be able to withstand the demands for penny fares, from Talbot Square to the No.3 Hotel in Devonshire Square, and from Central Station to Bloomfield Road, about which the residents are daily becoming more insistent. The Committee naturally wish to obtain all the long-distance fares possible. They would object to cars leaving Talbot Square full-up with penny fares, who would have to get-off by the No.3 Hotel, leaving the car to continue round Marton practically empty. It is too-much to expect short-distance passengers from Talbot Square or Central Station to pay as much as would take them to the Oxford Hotel. This is the point to which the Tramway Committee ought to direct their attention, and be of more-advantage to residents, who do not use these cars for pleasure purposes!

Evening Gazette

FAULTS OF THE NEW TRAMCARS - 24th April 1901

The new tramcars for the round Marton route are all very well to look at, in the glory of their fresh paint and varnish, but the more they are used the more their faults develop. The steps to enter the cars will - of course - have to be altered without delay, since they are eighteen inches from the ground - a ridiculous distance! It is not easy for the most-athletic to board the cars, but the feat will be almost impossible for obese or infirm persons, without considerable assistance being given them. Then the position of the life-guard - right underneath the car - makes it useless. Anyone who had the misfortune to be struck by the car would be very seriously hurt by the framework underneath, before getting anywhere near the lifeguard. The staircase also is awkward, while the closeness of the trellis-work round the top-deck, is not conducive to the comfort of those sitting against it. A space might have been left, in which passengers could rest their elbows. At present, a person sitting next to the railing, is forced to adopt rather an uncomfortable position. Why did the Tramway Committee, who went to Midland Carriage Works at Shrewsbury some time ago, not point-out these various defects? Surely it is the province of the designers, to study the comfort and convenience of passengers, in every possible detail? Even handsome fittings and elaborate workmanship do not excuse faults which may appear trifling, to the thousands of passengers who will use the cars each week.

Evening Gazette

MORE TRAMWAY EXTENSIONS - 14TH June 1901

Next winter there is to be further laying of new tramways. The Tramway Committee at their meeting yesterday, considered what developments were desirable, and decided upon two extensions. Firstly, the Layton line from Talbot Square is to be continued along Talbot Road and New Road as far as the Cemetery gates. This is to be a single route, and to form a penny-stage. Then a connection is to be made between the Lytham Road tramway and the new line around Marton, by way of Waterloo Road. From the corner of Central Drive to Lytham Road is only about five hundred yards, so this new line will not be a big job. For these extensions, and to meet emergencies on the other tram routes, the Committee have decided to order about twenty new tramcars. The question arose as to whether these cars should be a fixed-body four-wheeler or eight-wheel bogie-car type, similar to the large Promenade cars. The bogie-cars cost at least £300 more than the four-wheelers, but the Committee did decide to order these, as being more versatile in capacity.

Evening Gazette

A pleasant scene at the end of Raikes Road in Devonshire Square, showing two Marton Box-cars alongside at the tram stop, with the nearest being 28.
Barry Shaw

Opposite: *On the Circular Tour in Whitegate Drive, Toastrack 78 is fully-loaded and flying the Union Jack and the French Flag. Walking along the pavement beneath the new trees, is the postman delivering the mail.*
Author's Collection

Some Marton Dates to Remember

1900 - November 19 - Work commenced on the construction of the route, outside Marton Parish Church , where the crown of the hill was taken away, and the roadway was much widened.

1901 - May 20 - Trial-run made by an official party, and photograph taken in front of Oxford Hotel.

1901 - May 23 - Ministry inspection of the Marton route, obstructed in Abingdon street by two cycles carrying a banner between them and warning about the danger of new tram lines to cyclists!

1901 - November - trams could not enter Marton Depot because the track-fan had to be relaid and the building altered to accommodate them! The 15 Marton Box cars were kept in Blundell St depot.

1902 - April 28 - Clifton Street "cut-off" was constructed for the trams to enter Talbot Square, instead of via the full-length of Abingdon Street and Talbot Road, amongst the new Layton trams

1902 - August - The new line from Waterloo Hotel to Royal Oak was opened, so that the Marton route could operate to Victoria (South) Pier, in addition to Central Station via Central Drive.

1911 - August - Circular Tour introduced, using open toastracks and starting from Talbot Square - via Victoria Pier - Station Road - Royal Oak and the Marton route.

1912 - October - Marton depot enlarged to accommodate circa forty-eight trams.

1923 - June - the first of 42 Standard cars No.33 was produced in the Blackpool Tramway workshops.

1925 - The widening of the town-centre streets and the doubling of the tram tracks.

1929 - Vestibules constructed on sixteen Standard-cars to enclose the driver platforms, and a further sixteen were totally-enclosed and thus more-suitable for winter service.

1931 - By this time, there were 55 Standard-cars including new - and rebuilt from older types.

1936 - October 26 - closure of the Marton route along Central Drive to Central Station and the Layton route from Talbot Square to Layton Cemetery, which were replaced by new bus services.

1938 - Under the Thirties plan for the modernisation of the fleet, 15 new Balloon-cars were specially designed for the Marton route to replace the Standards, (but never constructed).

1939 - September - Second World War - the plan for modernisation was shelved and in November, Marton depot was requisitioned by the Air Ministry for aircraft production.

1940 - January - Heavy snowfalls resulted in several trams being left in drifts on the Marton route.

1944 - December - Marton depot de-requisitioned by the R.A.F. and restored for trams again with overhead installed, however a central air-raid shelter was retained!

1946 - Marton tram track in a very bad state of repair, and the future of the route was in-question, while the speed of trams was reduced for safety.`

1947 - January - Blackpool Council decided to relay the Marton tram track at a cost of £60,000.

1948 - Rehabilitated cars 10 - l5 were placed in service on the Marton route, jointly with Standards.

1949 - December - the first Marton Vambac 21 went into service, complete with modern equipment.

1951 - May 21 - 50th Anniversary of the Marton route - the depot was decorated with flags, and trams carried a special notice commemorating this occasion.

1952 - August 6 - at midnight new Coronation car 305 was tested between Talbot Square and Marton Depot. All 12 Marton Vambac cars 10 - 21 were then in-service, together with Vambac 208.

1952 - The last few service-Standards were replaced by six conventional English Electric railcoaches.

1957 - The Circular Tour was reintroduced via Squires Gate Lane and the Marton route.

1961 - October 29 - 205 was the last tram from South Pier to Marton, following closure of the Squires Gate route. In the 1962 season, all Marton trams terminated at Royal Oak.

1962 - October 28 - Ceremonies for the closure of the Marton Route with 48 from Royal Oak, 40 and illuminated 158 & 159 from Talbot Square. They had entered the depot by midnight!

Standards 41 and 28 seen at Beechfield Avenue on 14th January 1947 showing the worn track, just as a decision had been made for the future.
Evening Gazette

In the Talbot Square terminus separate from the traffic, Marton Vambac 20 awaits its departure for Royal Oak.
Author

Post-War Developments of the Marton Route

Undoubtedly the challenge of the post-war years for General Manager Walter Luff, centred on the Marton route, since in 1938 the Town Council had deferred its relaying and buying fifteen modern new trams. Of course he was keen on having a "super transport system", including diverting the Promenade tramway to the seaside of the Metropole Hotel and developing new trams in the style of the successful American PCC cars. The opening salvoes in the "Battle for Marton" were fired in January 1946, when reports on track renewal and alternative forms of transport were given by Walter Luff and the Borough Surveyor. This showed the Council that retaining Marton trams would cost £136,360 - £61,360 for track and £75,000 for fifteen new trams - while conversion to buses would cost £56,940 or trolleybuses £87,360, including road-reinstatement and rebuilding Marton depot. The Transport Manager concluded his report by favouring retention of the trams, advocating the introduction of those with resilient-wheels and high average speeds, so improving the street route. Here the virtues of the PCC cars were advocated for the first time, and Mr. Luff would have to work fast if he wanted the new "silent tram" to influence the course of events! While the Council considered the alternatives, the Gazette & Herald stated: "How could Blackpool possibly have carried-on during the six years of the War, without its tramways?" The Borough Surveyor was instructed to keep the Marton route in a state of reasonable repair, but undoubtedly former pupils of Blackpool Grammar School at Raikes Parade will remember how a noise of passing trams drowned the words of teachers!

A new generation of trams was the objective of Walter Luff, in convincing the Council to make the right decision. "A tram which by its sheer frequency and riding qualities could compete not just with the bus, but with its future competitor - the private car." Clearly he could foresee the developments in the post-war years! In March 1946, two new Maley & Taunton bogies with resilient-wheels and equipped with four Crompton Parkinson motors arrived in Blackpool, and Brush car 303 was fitted with them. Tests of this experimental car started in 1946, including the reserved-track of the Fleetwood route and more significantly, the badly worn track of the Marton route.

The BBC took sound recordings on April 26, travelling over the defective Marton route and finding that 303 was practically silent, compared with the ordinary Standard cars. It was described as having "velvet wheels" just gliding-along, while people on the street were surprised to see this tram going at full speed, without hearing it! In December, when railcoach 208 was fitted with the same new bogies, together with the "Vambac" (Variable Automatic Multinotch Braking & Acceleration Control) equipment, the Council was invited for a demonstration run showing what future-trams would be like. On January 8 1947, the Council decided by a narrow margin of 25 - 21 votes to have the Marton route relaid! Work commenced immediately, using 600 tons of new rail and also point-work, while throughout the three-mile route, railjoints were Thermit-welded. At this time, the service cars were operating single-line during the relaying, with their trolleys at an angle - facilitated by swivel-heads!

In mid-1947 prototype 208 was ready for service, but did not appear on the Marton route. Trials were held, including testing the curve into Abingdon Street and training drivers to familiarise them with its performance, sitting to drive and thrusting the joystick forward for acceleration and pulling it back for deceleration. Thus the drivers found it more comfortable, and one said: "This car is so quiet that the holidaymakers on the Prom can't hear you coming!" At this time, a decision was made about ordering new trams for the Marton route, and since manufacturing costs were rising beyond the budget, it was decided that twelve sun-saloons of 1939 would be rebuilt and re-equipped with the successful "Vambac". Late in 1947, eighteen sets of bogies and equipment were ordered, and work started in re-fitting "Marton Vambacs" 10 - 21. On 18 January 1948, 10 became the first modern car on the Marton route, contrasting in appearance with the double-deck Standards. The centre-roof panelling was fitted with fluorescent lighting, new partitions for the driver-cabs, moquette seats, and finished in a new livery with a smart flare at each end! When 21 appeared in December 1949 - the first fitted with Vambac equipment - it proved able to operate more swiftly than the Standards. When all twelve and 208 were at Marton in 1952, the Standards covered "school-specials", and were finally phased-out of service when more than six railcoaches arrived. These were sadly lacking their planned Vambac equipment, which was being used as "spares" for the twenty-five new and unpredictable Coronation cars!

Seen from the office of the Winter Gardens is Marton Vambac 13, turning into Church Street with Burton's Cafe, Sweet & Clarke's and the new Timothy White's Chemist in the background.
Colin McLeod

A view from the photographer's flat, seeing railcoach 205 passing. It is following Ribble Atlantean, which is advertising "ITS BEST BY BUS" as a warning to trams!
Colin McLeod

It was somewhat ironic that pioneer Brush car 303 did not go into service on the Marton route, since during trials in 1946 conductors found that the air-doors were too slow. Having been re-equipped with a spare Vambac, it returned to its native Bispham Depot where it was unpopular with the drivers, and made infrequent appearances! Following the departure of the traditional Standards from the Marton route in 1952, it was worked by the Vambac cars with some railcoaches, and had become efficient. The local passengers found that it was the finest tram service ever offered, with smooth riding single-deckers which appeared every three minutes! In the Fifties, traffic was quiet and there was no problem for the passengers boarding trams in the streets. At Talbot Square, the tram terminus was isolated from the traffic by islands, and at Royal Oak in 1956 the same was provided for the alighting passengers. Since the passengers liked the new "Marton Vambacs", so did the platform staff and especially the drivers who found them simple to drive. It was true, that as trams accelerated away from stops, they could leave buses behind. In 1949, experiments carried out with 208 found that it could reach 30 mph in 17 seconds, whereas a bus took 23 seconds! Also the Vambac equipment provided smooth and swift-braking down to a speed of 2 mph, the drivers then using the air-brakes to halt the car. The daily appearance of cars 10 - 21 on the Marton route proved that they were successful. This confirmed the effectiveness of the routine maintenance in the depot, inspecting the rotary accelerator which was positioned beneath the trolley tower. It became interesting that Walter Luff claimed that trams featuring new bogies with resilient-wheels represented a saving in track costs, and would ensure a life of 30 years for the new track of Marton. Other cars travelling along this track, en-route for the Promenade as "Specials", contrasted in being noisy on the track, much to the annoyance of the local residents. Today, it is interesting to reflect upon the unique status of the Marton route in Britain, and similar involvement during 1947 of the Glasgow and Leeds City tramway systems. Each of them had a trial car with Vambac equipment - Leeds Roe-built single-decker 602 and Glasgow double-deck Cunarder 1005. Alas, hopes of such a modern fleet for their systems, were dashed by the decision to abandon their tramways in 1959 and 1962 respectively. Thus Blackpool remained a pioneer of tramway development in the Twentieth-Century!

A delightful scene on Whitegate Drive, showing Vambac 13 passing Beechfield Avenue and with little traffic rivalling the tram in its prime position.
Colin McLeod

With its demise in 1962, the Marton Experiment can still be stated as a success, even though by example - performance, silent-running, ease-of-control, routine maintenance, and saving of track-wear - did not induce any other tramways to invest in similar equipment. Clearly in other cities, tramway closure was tempted by the attractive cheapness of bus-operation. In Blackpool, the new equipment did all that its manufacturer claimed for it, and after initial trials continued to function smoothly and efficiently for more than twelve years. The manufacturers - Crompton-Parkinson and Maley & Taunton - with Vambac & HS44 combination, represented the ultimate development of street tramway practice in this country, with superior qualities of both riding and silence in movement. As for its popularity with the public, one only needs to mention that when the abandonment was first proposed in 1961, there was a very considerable outcry from the population served. Marton residents organised a massive petition to the Town Council for its retention, and without any prompting from tramway enthusiasts! The campaign was headed by Ald.J.S.Richardson who - as Mayor of Blackpool - had to preside at its closing ceremonies on Sunday 28th October 1962. Why then did the Marton route close, and where did the experiment fail? The answer sadly lies in the economic impossibility of two man operation with small 48-seat trams, once the passengers began to decline. Also, there are three subsidiary factors to be cited. First, there was the cost of spare-parts, which in an unique situation for the manufacturers, must have been high. Secondly, the high energy costs arose from the 4-motor Vambac cars, starting from rest in-parallel and thus swiftly accelerating. Thirdly, the increasingly difficult relationship between trams and other road users by 1960, which included unfamiliar drivers entering Blackpool. Ultimately, the high ratio of staff to passengers had brought about the demise of the Marton route, since crew costs accounted for nearly 75% of the transport budget. Since other tramway costs were higher than those of buses, the way to off-set them included high-loading factors as with the double-deck cars on the busy Promenade. Of course, ten years after the closure of Marton, in 1972 Blackpool Transport introduced OMO cars to the Fleetwood route for economy of operation. If only Walter Luff had introduced them - like the American PCCs - in 1946, the Marton route could have survived. After its sad closure, it took thirty years in Britain before trams returned to streets, first in Manchester, followed by Sheffield, Birmingham and Croydon. So it is true that the Marton street route in Blackpool has provided inspiration for the future!

A busy scene of the Marton trams in Talbot Square with two railcoaches, and many pedestrians free to walk across the roads in 1962!
Colin McLeod

Do You Remember the Marton Route?

Whilst this is not a complete history of the Marton route, it is a personal recollection of riding on the trams through the centre of Blackpool and away from the familiar Promenade trams, along the unique street route here. Now we have entered a new Millennium, the Marton tram route certainly belongs to the Twentieth-century, starting in 1901 and finishing on 28th October 1962. Readers who lived in those years may recall stepping out into the road and boarding the tram - to Talbot Square or Royal Oak - and South Pier during the summer months. For the younger generation today it may seem hard to imagine, although the Blackpool & Fleetwood coastal-line travels through the main streets at the north end, and a new generation of trams have returned to British cities.

Passengers leaving Vambac 20 at Honister Avenue stop, with an approaching tram passing the Marton Parish Church. In the foreground is a warning school-sign, with Saddle Inn and Marton Depot in the background.
Colin McLeod

I am sure that nobody will remember the first car stopping at the Oxford Hotel on the trial run of the Marton trams in 1901, or riding on the first Circular Tours in 1911, for the simple reason that most of us were not born at the time! Neither shall we recall the little open-top Marton "Box-cars", or the later "De-Luxe" cars with rattan seats and curtained windows of the saloon. Most of us will associate the Marton route with the Standard double-deck cars - built in Blackpool during the Twenties - with hard wooden seats upstairs and upholstered sprung seats in the saloon. In some cars with longitudinal seats at each side, passengers gazed at each other over string-bags of weekend shopping and it could be an apology for comfort! At busy periods, standing passengers held on to the strap-hangers downstairs, to avoid losing their footing as the car swayed along the route. Everyone went by tram in the post-war years, except the more exclusive wealthy people, and before the arrival of the Morris Minor and Austin Mini cars. Yes, the tram had the monopoly of the road, from the centres of Church Street, Whitegate Drive with its trees and curves, and Waterloo Road. Motor traffic could overtake on the inside of the tram, until it was halted by the extended arm of the conductor to indicate departing passengers. In those post-war years, having travelled along the Promenade on one of the railcoaches with upholstered seats and a centre entrance, when one crossed the road into Talbot Square at the Marton tram terminus, there was no mistake that you were back in the pre-war years of the Twenties and the Thirties. There would stand two imposing green and cream Standards, one with an open-balcony and one fully enclosed, both with their steps hanging invitingly from their high wooden platforms. Their trolleys were usually crossed, and one always hoped - and yet dreaded - that a calamity would occur - but it never - or rarely did. The crew always remembered to turn their trolley and ensure it was on the correct overhead line, before each car swept out with the dignity of a duchess, rumbling over the points with a thunderous noise, before swaying gently up Clifton Street.

A view from Hunter's Shop showing Balloon 252 turning into Abingdon Street, after being a Promenade "Special" that day.   **Colin McLeod**

The scene in Devonshire Square, with Boat 225 following Standard 40 to Marton depot, and watched by the queue for town at the tram stop opposite!
Author

For myself - as a child - I always wanted to ride on the open-tram, with its spacious balcony and a commanding position, from which one could watch other trams swing into view round a bend of the road, approach with a notorious pitching and rolling, and sweep past bearing another load of shoppers into the town. "CARS STOP BY REQUEST" proclaims the circular tram stop - and a crowd of people would step determinedly into the road with arms raised for our car to stop. "Hold Tight", came the cry from the conductor, as the last passenger grasped the hand-rail and put his foot on the platform step. "Ting" went the bell, a rattle as the driver released the hand-brake, and the car moved slowly forward and then more quickly as the "click-click" of the controller reached the top-notch of parallel. The motor booming at first, developed a howling noise as the tram moved forward over the shining rails below, at a seemingly fast rate. The trolley boom echoed the "swish" as the trolley head negotiated the "frogs" and the ears of the span-wires. This enthralling routine was often repeated before the cry of "Stanley Park" was heard from the conductor below, and I grabbed the seat backs to keep my balance before being precipitated down the curved stairs. The passengers pushed past the conductor with his hands on the bell rope, impatiently awaiting our departure into the street below. The smell of pies sizzling on the hot resistances under the stairs for the crew, assailed our nostrils before stepping off the step of the car, and breathing the clean fresh air once again. The Standard tram, "like a raucous swan of steel", departed over the rails of Whitegate Drive, round the next bend and so disappeared from view.

On my return journey, after a delightful day spent in Stanley Park, I waited with bated breath to see whether the next car to appear round the corner would be my favourite Standard or one of the "new trams", which by 1948 were being introduced to the Marton route to replace them. Of course, by this time the Marton route was being relaid and for the future needed modern cars to supply a three-minute service. However, in those days I was always prepared to let a modern car go past and wait for a ride on a Standard, experiencing the delight of being swung from one side of the car to the other, whilst firmly gripping the strap-hanger and apologising for treading on the toes of those who sat near me. I have to admit that once I was embarrassed, since having fallen into the pond at Stanley Park, my clothes were wet and consequently dripped on to the floor of the tram. The conductor thus made me stand under the stairs, out of the way! There were several stops before the terminus, and when the car rolled into Talbot Square the driver, having wound-up the brake-handle with the ratchet in, would then release the hand brake column with a deafening rattle. Thus he seemingly allowed the car to stop itself. Sad to relate, the Standards disappeared from the Marton service in 1952, by which time it became characterised by the single deck Vambac cars, distinguished by their pointed fronts and modern equipment. Undoubtedly this was the achievement of General Manager Walter Luff, who was keen to prove that in post-war years Blackpool demonstrated the success of an efficient street tram route. There were twelve Marton Vambacs and a converted railcoach 208, which should have been joined by a further six of this type. However, six conventional railcoaches arrived in 1952, when preoccupation was with the new Coronation cars on the Promenade and Fleetwood service.

A traditional sight of balcony-car 40 in Whitegate Drive, showing "TALBOT SQUARE via MARTON" on its indicator. **Author**

Passengers leaving Standard 147 in Talbot Square, while the service-car waits to leave. **Author**

Since the abandonment of the Layton and Central Drive routes in 1936, the Marton street route remained exclusive amongst the Blackpool tram routes, being completely independent of them and operating from Marton Depot. Certainly this reflected the more traditional British tramway practice and became more distinctive, as the National tramway empire diminished in the Fifties. To the tramway enthusiasts, Marton Depot situated in Whitegate Drive near to the historic Saddle Inn, was of great interest as it housed the distinctive depleted ranks of the Standards, the twelve open Boat cars, and a selection of Illuminated cars, Television cars and even restored historic cars. Marton Depot had always been a "must" for visiting tramway enthusiasts, who had been eager to peer through its open doors, or explore its darkest recesses with permission. I can never forget once finding open-top car Southampton 45 there, which had been saved in 1949 by L.R.T.L. members. It founded the Tramway Museum Society, by being handed over to them here on 29th May 1955! The depot office was always cosy, with a fire burning in a grate and the inspector and his reserves swapping tales, between counting cash. Here the crew paid-in their takings, and always referred to the route as the "Copper Canyon". It is true that the Marton crews retained the friendly atmosphere of their depot, knowing each other by name, along with their route and its regular passengers. In addition to the twelve regular service cars, were three school specials which latterly used double-deck Balloon cars, reflecting the many schools which lined the route. In the summer season Marton Depot supplied the Boat-cars for the Promenade and for the famous Circular Tour, which reached its finale in 1961 when the Squires Gate route closed. In 1956 during the Illuminations, I went with my friends to catch one of the Standards, leaving the depot for performing the Illuminations Tours on the Promenade. We rode down Waterloo Road to Royal Oak, and along Lytham Road to the huge queue for tours at the Tower. Being on the balcony of Standard 40, we were allowed to remain there for a Tour of the Illuminations, and consequently I shall never forget it! In the street outside the depot was an interwoven fan of point-work and rail, set in the traditional cobbles. Usually a tram stood there, waiting for a change-over crew or the traditional "brew". This was a fine tradition and worth recording today, for the younger generations.

Looking from Thomas's Ford showroom is seen Vambac-car 13 with the allotments behind, as it approaches Oxford Square. **Colin McLeod**

Railcoach 207 seen on the railway bridge outside South Station, with Waterloo Road behind it and a service-car heading for Marton. In September 1962, 207 from Bispham Depot was new to the route! **Author**

If, on a Marton tram ride, we had kept our eyes on the overhead, instead of the track in front, we would have seen a number of features worthy of note. The trolley reverser at Royal Oak was always a source of fascination, as one watched the trolley of the reversing tram swing out sideways and then recede to its rightful position behind it, just as it climbed the railway bridge and disappear from view. Also interesting to note were the spans of catenary suspension to the overhead, outside the Waterloo Road School, possibly designed for future pantographs! Before the junction of Hornby Road and Whitegate Drive there was a "skate" in the overhead to operate the traffic lights, while one outside Yates's Wine Lodge operated the points for the terminus lines in Talbot Square. Yes, Marton had its individuality as a tram route, which we all missed when the buses took over on the 29th October 1962. The sights of a driver swinging the trolley of his car in Talbot Square, a driver getting out of his cab in Clifton Street to find the owner of a car parked over the rails, and a Marton Vambac car nosing into the curve of Abingdon Street - one of the sharpest on the system - are memorable! Other sights of the Marton trams included their swinging round the broad curve in front of the Winter Gardens, sweeping round the curve at Oxford Square, and poised on the top of the South Station bridge, waiting for another car to clear the terminus at Royal Oak. In the summer season every third car travelled to South Pier via Lytham Road and Station Road, thus employing a point-boy to ensure the right direction for the trams at Royal Oak! Now, all these sights of trams in these locations are gone forever, can you remember - or imagine - them?

The End of an Era – 1962

Of course, some of us will recall the closure of the last British street tram route, here in Blackpool on 28th October 1962. That weekend marked a significant gathering of the national tramway enthusiasts to participate in its finale. By this time, the locals had formed a Tramway Historical Association, published a Tramway News and presented a Tramway Exhibition on the last weekend of the Marton route. Situated in the Revoe Library on the former Central Drive tram route, it was visited by hundreds of enthusiasts and the local public. Certainly the model layout, combined with a display of nostalgic historic views, proved to be attractive. This was coupled with riding on the Marton route for the last time on Sunday, and naturally three tours were organised, twice using Standard 48 and also Standard 40 together with Brush-car 300, providing some memorable experiences. There was no doubt about it, we traversed as much of the Marton route as possible using crossovers in many locations, but we did not fail to notice the new bus stops in position, judiciously covered to conceal the impending fate of the tramway. On this last day, the track proved to be in good condition, but it was hard to imagine that we could never again ride on trams here. Being Sunday, there was only a nine-minute service, using six cars - Marton Vambacs 11, 13, 15, 17 & 18 and Railcoach 217. There were thirty-four trams in Marton Depot on that day, including the remaining Vambacs, Railcoaches, Standards and Boat cars, comprising the Marton tramway family.

While we made the most of Marton route's last hours to ride on the speedy and smooth Marton Vambacs, and thus experienced the surge of acceleration and braking over the smooth track. We knew that the last journeys from each end of the route - Talbot Square & Royal Oak - would be made respectively by traditional Standards 40 and 48. Thus they would replace the Marton Vambacs 13 & 11 on their last journeys, and using the same crews! By 10 p.m. some of us visited Marton Depot, to see preparations well under-way for the Farewell Party of the native crews. There was a splendid cake and refreshments prepared, but sadly the depot cat had made an early departure, and was commemorated by its plate on the wall! Amongst the lines of silent trams in the depot, Standard 40 was at the front waiting to take over from Vambac 13 on the final journey to Talbot Square. Next was Standard 48, which would replace Vambac 11 to Royal Oak at 11-21 p.m., and was decorated by a wreath and a placard reading "Royal Oak's Last Tram". So the curtain rose on the final scene.

Standard 48 is seen at Rectory Road on the last day's tour. Notice the covered bus-stop. **Author**

Vambac 11 is seen outside Marton Depot, on its last journey to Talbot Square. **Author**

"Royal Oak's Very Last Tram" 48 enters the depot finally!   **Author**

40 arrives from Talbot Square, crowded with enthusiasts!   **Author**

When the time came, the two Standards were standing outside the depot waiting for the last journey, and as the last Vambacs arrived their passengers transferred for a final ride. As they set off in opposite direction along Whitegate Drive, they looked picturesque recreating the traditional scene. Some of us chose 48 for Royal Oak, and the ride on such a crowded car was like many last tram rides in other cities. The car travelled at a good-pace along Waterloo Road without stopping, and then slowly climbed the railway bridge at South Station. Once 48 had been photographed as the last tram ever to be at Royal Oak, the bell was rung by the conductor and being fully loaded it struggled up the hill! The driver sounded the gong several times, signalling farewell to Royal Oak for ever. We returned along Waterloo Road at some speed, passing the lighted windows of the houses, and approached Spen Corner. As the tram lurched round the curve, with its wheel grating in the track, someone even cried "We're off" but we were not, and continued at speed to Oxford Square. Here the original first car had stopped in 1901, but on this final occasion the landlord and staff of the Oxford Hotel stood on the steps and waved as we passed, watching the last tram disappear for ever. As we approached Marton Depot, we could see a crowd had gathered to see the last tram ceremony, and significantly two new buses - Leyland PD3s - were parked in front of the depot, waiting for the official party. "Everybody out" called the conductor and we left 48, watching it crossover and enter the depot for the last time!

MARTON becomes NOTRAM!

Standard 40 then arrived from Talbot Square packed with enthusiasts on its balcony, and it was their turn to dismount and join the crowd. Once 40 was empty it inched slowly through the crowd and was framed in the doorway, captured by a shower of flashlights. Finally the radiant sight of fully-illuminated 158 appeared round the curve and approached the waiting crowd. The trolley was swung on to the depot approach-line, as the passengers left and 158 was cheered inside. Then the finale arrived, as illuminated 159 appeared in its own halo and approached the cheering crowd. Unfortunately there was a mishap with the trolley pole de-wiring and the lights went out, but the shed-man recovered it while the Mayor Ald J.S. Richardson left the car, and walked toward the buses. 159 moved slowly towards the depot doors, was lit-up by flash-lights, cheered by the crowd and the depot doors were closed behind it. The official guests left by two buses for a reception at the Transport Office, the depot staff started their party, and the crowd dispersed. We looked up at the nearest traction-pole where the new bus stop was fixed next to the "All Cars Stop Here" tram stop. As a person remarked: "In reverse Marton has become Notram, after all!"

A dramatic scene at Marton Depot as illuminated Standard 158 enters, and the crowd look towards the final 159!　　　　　**Author**

The National Tramway Museum

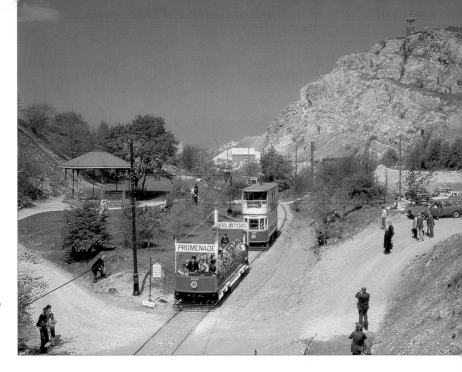

A delightful scene at Crich in 1984, looking from the bridge towards the Crich Stand, showing Blackpool cars - Toastrack 166 and Standard 40 - both in red and white livery.
Author

Standard 49 in the attractive green-and-cream livery, seen in the cobbled depot yard at Crich, along with the rail-crane. Nostalgically, its indicator is showing "PLEASURE BEACH & CLIFTON DRIVE".
Author

Following the closure of the Marton route and depot, along with the other street routes, the National Tramway Museum at Crich was offered the vintage restored cars 1, 2, 40 & 59, together with Standards 40 & 49 and Pantograph 167. Having collected trams from the closing city systems of Leeds, Sheffield and Glasgow, they had to refuse the further offer of the pioneer Railcoach 200 and Vambac 11. In 1964, Tramroad cars 2 and 40 were the first to operate under power at Crich, followed by many other cars, including 40, 49 & Dreadnought 59. Subsequently, the total of Blackpool trams rose to ten, with the addition of Grinder 2, Toastrack 166 and Brush-car 298. It has been fascinating that 40 and 167 were loaned back to Blackpool for the Promenade-line Centenary in 1985, then Box 40 twice - in 1988 & 1996 - plus 2 and 167 for the Tramroad Centenary in 1998. Undoubtedly, NTM has to be awarded the credit for the salvation of the vintage Blackpool fleet and their operation in a charming setting!

Finale of
the Standards

Following the closure of the Marton route, four Standards continued in use on the Promenade. 160 is seen on Central Promenade in 1964, as a useful "Special" with 78 seats and needing only one conductor. Sadly, this car was broken up in April 1967 providing equipment spares for Engineering-car 3.
Author

A solo-view of 147 on the Pleasure Beach loop in 1966, looking rusty but still being handsome in appearance, as the last conventional Standard-car here.
Author

The East Anglia Transport Museum

Standard 159 appears emerging from the woods at the Museum, while still showing MARTON on its indicator. Seen in 1982, it has been re-painted but does not yet include the gold lining. **R.P. Fergusson**

Marton Vambac 11 seen in service, and looking exactly as it did on its native route in Blackpool. It is however showing the unusual destination of FLEETWOOD - 1. **R.P. Fergusson**

This museum was founded at Carlton Colville in 1965, and has included wide ranging examples of street transport, including the electrical trolley buses and trams. From the Marton Depot family is Standard 159, which arrived in 1967 and was restored, together with unique Vambac 11. In this case, it was remarkable that this car was extracted from Marton Depot in January 1963 for a final tour with the vintage cars, and did not return! It went to Havant in Kent for a new light-rail scheme on Hayling Island, which did not materialise and consequently EATMS acquired it in 1969. It operated in service for several years, until it was decided that it should be restored for both its body and the Vambac equipment. It is hoped that this will be completed in 2001, and will appear in the original livery as used on the Marton route, in post-war years.

Standard 144 loaded for its final departure to the U.S.A. and showing "North Station Blackpool"   **Evening Gazette**

Blackpool Trams in the U.S.A.   STANDARD 144

The first departure of a tram from Blackpool to the U.S.A. took place by Standard 144 at 2-30 pm on 11th March 1955. The story began in September 1953, when Dwight B. Minnich - Assistant General Manager of the Seashore Line - made contact with the L.R.T.L. Museum Committee. They were interested in acquiring a London tram, but found that they were too late, since all the London trams had been scrapped, following the closure in 1952. Keith Pearson of the Museum Committee informed them of the historic cars still in existence in 1954, and illustrated them with photographs. Thus their interest was created in Blackpool, where Keith provided a survey of the "beautifully kept" Standard-cars in Marton Depot, of which he identified balcony-car 144 as "particularly sound". It was suggested to Mr. Minnich that he approach General Manager J.C. Franklin, with a view to obtaining Standard 144 for the Seashore line at Kennebunkport. At its meeting on 22nd October 1955, Blackpool Transport Committee agreed to present Standard 144, complete in running-order and free-of-charge, to Seashore Electric Railway. Thus it was first arranged for 144 to be shipped from Liverpool to Boston, as deck-cargo with separated upper and lower decks, but finally in the form of complete-body stowage in the hold. The departure of 144 on 11th March - advertising Blackpool as a Holiday Resort - was arranged by Lep Transport, and witnessed by the Blackpool Mayor, Chairman of the Transport Committee - Ald. Rhodes Marshall - and Manager J.C.Franklin. At Liverpool Docks on 15th March, Mammoth - the Mersey Docks and Harbour Board floating-crane - lifted 144's body and lowered it with precision into the hold of the United States Lines ship "American Press". The bogies had been separately loaded, and the ship sailed for Boston on Sunday 20th March.

It arrived in East Boston at midnight on 28th March, and on the next day unloading 144 commenced, with the bogies being lifted off by a lighter-boat crane, but the body was more difficult to extract, as it had been set on the port side of the ship's hold. Thus it had to be slid on skids, turned ready to be lifted out of the hold, and then placed on a lighter-boat, which moved it to another pier. Meanwhile Seashore had made intensive preparations for this unique acquisition of a tram from the U.K., and sent a tractor and two trailers to the harbour-pier of Boston. Having been loaded by the lighter-crane, the bogies were first taken to Seashore, while 144's body on a long trailer was stored in a compound and guarded overnight - by a policeman! On the next day the difficult journey commenced, since the height of the tram and trailer amounted to 17 ft 6 ins, while the Boston trolleybus overhead was 18ft high. Since this would vary - notably at heavy junctions - a sheet of plywood was attached to the front of 144's roof, and a member of the moving-crew travelled on the open-balcony to ensure the overhead slid over the roof! At one place it did separate twin-wires for the distance of several span-wires, until they were free. Once it was out of the City and away from the overhead, further problems were encountered by the low height of the flyovers on the highways, involving manoeuvres. The distance of 75 miles was covered by the night, and on Saturday 2nd April 144 was unloaded on to supporting blocks. On Sunday 10th April, 144 was reunited with its bogies, and when Seashore's power-plant was restored, 144 was driven under power again and she performed very well! The overhead of the museum had to be raised to 18 feet at several points of the museum line, and guard-rails were added to the curves to ensure 144 maintained the track.

On board Mersey Docks & Harbour Board crane "Mammoth", 144 is about to be lifted on to the ship "American Press", for its voyage to Boston. The Liverpool Overhead Railway can be seen behind.   **F.K. Pearson**

Seashore Trolley Museum

Loaded with passengers at Seashore, 144 is now painted in the red and white livery, with the exception of its bogies, lifeguards and ticket boxes, which are still in green - with its native address!
Joseph M. Williams

Thus Blackpool Standard 144 became Seashore's most popular exhibit in 1955, since clearly it was the only double-deck tram there. After some time in the open, 144 was then stored in Seashore's new depot, and was repainted in the earlier pre-1933 livery of red and white. Details were supplied by Blackpool Transport Department, and thus lining was applied, although correctly, gold lining should have been used on the lower panels and its number in the same style. However the Corporation crest was retained, and the name-and-address of the original operator! In the forty-five years since l44's arrival, it has remained in service longer than it was in Blackpool, where it was built in 1924! Undoubtedly this was a fine example of a Blackpool car in the U.S.A., and it was subsequently followed by a further two Standards - 48 & 147 - and ultimately three Boat cars - 226, 228 & 606 - thus keeping our flag flying there!

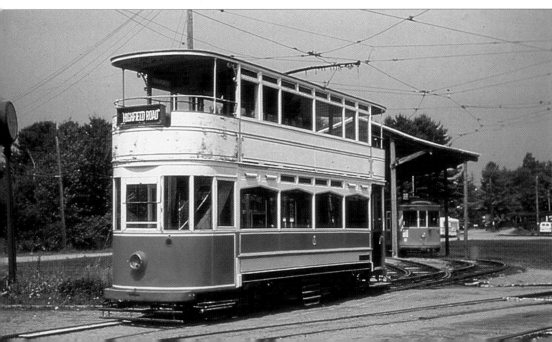

In 1990, 144 still looks handsome, but ready for repainting again! At Seashore, it will never reach its "Highfield Road" destination again!
Ian M. Dougill

27

48 Started a New Life in America – 1964

Contributed by Roy E. Bonn, former General Manager of Willamette Shore Trolley.

The story of Standard 48's journey to America really began in August 1962, when the tram was still in use as a "special" on Blackpool Promenade, operating from Marton Depot. At that time the closure of the Marton tram route would take place on 28th October, and it was heard in America that Blackpool Transport was planning to scrap the double-deck Standard trams. A letter was sent by Paul Class of O.E.R.H.S. to General Manager J.C.Franklin: "Our purpose in writing is to ask for preserving a Blackpool Standard double-deck tram, in the same way as your Standard 144 at Seashore Trolley Museum, Maine, U.S.A.". The General Manager of Blackpool Transport replied by a letter dated August 31st 1962: "Sometime in the near future we may be taking some of our old double-deck trams out of service, and you can rest assured that your inquiry will receive the consideration of the Transport Committee. I am sure that they would be happy to donate one of our Standard cars to your Museum free-of-charge." On March 21st 1963 a letter was received by the Society offering 48 to us, and after a poll by the Board of Trustees, a letter of acceptance was returned to J.C.Franklin on 12th April 1963. A considerable amount of time and effort was then carried out to bring Standard 48 from Blackpool to Oregon, along with the co-operation of A.K.Terry of the National Tramway Museum of Britain. Standard 48 was transported to the port of Hull, from which it left on August 28th l964, and became deck-cargo on the East Asiatic Company ship "M.V. Sibonga".

As destined for Portland, Oregon, "M.V. Sibonga" had scheduled-stops in the Virgin Islands - for 6th & 7th September - before the Panama Canal took the ship to the east side of America. The next stop was San Diego on 18th and Long Beach later on the same day. San Francisco was the next port of call on 23rd and finally Portland for September 26th, and so Blackpool 48 had become a real world-traveller! "MV Sibonga" docked at 7 p.m. on a beautiful Fall-evening, and 48 was sitting on the aft-end of the deck. The cover that had originally protected the body had been removed at one of the previous ports. The bogies and the lifeguards were brought up from the hold and placed next to 48's body, and it was unloaded at 10 p.m. and placed on to a truck. The shipment cleared Customs immediately, as the paperwork duties had been completed in advance, and the body was chained to the truck, which was driven from the dock and parked in a yard nearby. The bogies were loaded on to the "Old Blue" - the Societies' truck - and chained to it! It was then moved next to the body, and awaited the trip to Trolley Park on the following morning.

Sunday 27th September turned out to be a beautiful Fall Day, with clear blue skies and warm temperature. The height of the load was 19ft 6ins, which required 48 to be routed round several overpasses on Sunset Highway, and power and telephone cables were raised by utility crews in order to clear the route for Glenwood. All this was basically a devious route transported by the truck to Portland for use on the Willamette Shore Railway line demonstration project that Fall. The time of arrival was 2 p.m. and Paul Class rode in the upper-deck of 48, with a direct phone-line to the driver of the truck! He thus acted as the lookout to spot any obstructions and alert the driver! Quite separately it had been possible to drive "Old Blue" with the bogies directly to Glenwood, and the workshop crane was used for unloading and placing them on the rails. The axle-boxes and mounting-bolsters of the bogies were oiled, cleaned and the motors checked before the body would be mounted upon them again. Upon arrival, 48's body was lifted and the truck driven from underneath it, temporary track was built under the body and the the bogies were thus rolled into place. After some manoeuvring of the track and thus the bogies, which were not aligned properly, by 11 p.m. the body was finally lowered on to its bogies, being reunited for the first time since it left Blackpool! This had been a long but very satisfying day and then Key System car 159 (not a Standard!) was used to pull 48 under a trolley wire, the pole was raised and the lights shone - making a fine sight!

Willamette Shore Trolley

A dramatic scene as 48 is lifted on to Willamette Shore Railway track, from the Railroad track on which still stands its power-generator.
Roy E. Bonn

However the motors had yet to be connected, and various repairs and adjustments were required, as the car had been out of service - since its last journey from Marton to Blundell Street Depot on March 11th 1963 - for over twelve months. Some damage had occurred on the voyage over, as well as wear-and-tear from the many years of service in a coastal climate. I imagine that thousands of people had ridden on the car, during its many years of operation in Blackpool. The first publicity created by Standard 48 was in the Forest Grove News Times newspaper, and its reporter was waiting for its arrival at the Trolley Park on the Sunday, so it was pictured in the following week. During this time 48 was cleaned both inside and out, and all items which had been stowed inside the car for the voyage were unpacked. Such items as red quarter-lights, destinations blinds, light bulbs and the reverser-key were reinstalled, and other repairs were required. Electrical wires were connected, circuits were checked, and several tests were made prior to it going into revenue service. On Sunday 4th October 1964, 48 rolled out of the workshop and carried its first revenue passengers in the U.S.A. - on the 2 p.m. run. A total of four trips were operated, and $4 in donations were received. During the first years of operation at Glenwood, admission to Trolley Park was free and income was received in the form of donations from the public. Undoubtedly this represented a considerable achievement, and 48 has now been owned for 37 years, which is longer than it operated in Blackpool!

In November 1995, 48 was operated over the Portland & Western Railroad from Banks to Oswego - a distance of 30 miles - which was more sensible than the highway, where bridges have clearance of only 14 feet - or less! Here it was lifted on to Willamette Shore Railway track, which is parallel with the freight railroad for half-a-mile. The Trolley Line runs for seven miles between Portland and Lake Oswego, along the western side of the Willamette River. Two high trestles provide spectacular views overlooking the river, and the track continues through the 1,396 foot long Elk Rock Tunnel, making a gradual "S" curve between the portals. The line continues south through the woods as it wends its way to Lake Oswego, where the depot is in State Street.

AN INCOMPARABLE TROLLEY RIDE!

This unusual journey for a Blackpool double-decker provides a great novelty for the American passengers! Since the arrival of 48 at Portland in November 1995, the passengers have increased dramatically, and it has been used at weekends in summer to handle the crowds - having 78 seats. Passengers prefer to ride on 48, even though the ride is not as smooth as the Brill Master Unit 813. Of course there is no trolley overhead on this line, and 48 is driven by a generator unit which provides power for its motors. Although the appearance of Standard 48 retains its traditional livery, some basic changes have been made to carpet the lower saloon, thus replacing the wooden-batten floors. The platform entrances have smooth floors, as they were replaced during rebuilding in the Eighties. The lower saloon was restored to its original wood-finish, after the removal of many layers of varnish. Since entering service on the Willamette Shore Trolley line, 48 has required increased maintenance work. In December 1995, the motor-bearing on the south-end had to be replaced and some electrical wiring replaced on the motor. We discovered that the motors still had cotton-covered windings, and these had not been used in the U.S.A. for fifty years! The motor on the north end of 48 failed in September 1997, and was replaced by a spare-motor that we had in stock. Of course, the brake-shoes are replaced regularly due to the number of miles that 48 operated, together with the crossings and street running involved. There is a local foundry that produces brake-shoes for us from the Society-owned patterns. Heavy maintenance was scheduled for later in 1998, after the completion of the maintenance facility at the Willamette Shore Trolley. Repainting of 48's exterior was scheduled, as it had been sitting outdoors for the first three years there. Certainly the operating of any wooden framed car over jointed-rails has increased the amount of maintenance work, which is required to keep the body tight fitting. Of course, it has been intended to maintain its original appearance.

48 is Seen approaching Lake Oswego on the Portland & Western Railroad, two miles west of the car-barn.   **Roy E. Bonn**

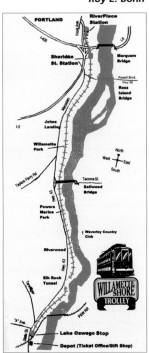

An attractive view as 48 emerges from the Elk Rock Tunnel showing its lights. **David J. Haynes**

48 is seen at John's Landing in 1996, with Lake Oswego in the background. **David J. Haynes**

I am sure that readers will be aware of the tremendous wear that the tram body takes, when operated over uneven tracks. Incidentally during the Eighties the exterior side wooden panels were removed and replaced by steel sheets, in American practice! During the last months of 2000, various maintenance tasks on 48 have been undertaken, including extensive repairs to the two controllers. A new roof canvas has been installed again this year, since the one fitted in the Eighties suffered with cracks, caused by the hard finish of the paint applied. Clearly the result was a leaking roof, and also the damage inflicted by low hanging tree branches. The sides have been re-sanded, and the entire car has been spray painted in the maintenance facility at Lake Oswego. Here the car-barn has two tracks, so that both cars - 48 and 813 - are stored indoors out of the weather, except when in operation. Also new brake-shoes were fitted, which is a yearly job owing to the amount of braking required at all the street crossings on this 7-mile rail line. In November the bogies were completely dismantled and inspected, during which the tyre-widening was rewelded, turned on a lathe, and rebuilt motors installed. They were then assembled, in time for the Christmas holiday charters.

Of the two cars in service at Willamette Shore Trolley, Brill Master-unit 813 is usually operated, when the weather is cold and heat is required for passenger comfort. Car 48 is used during the summer months, and both cars operate when large crowds are carried, or when required for charter-service. On holidays, such as Christmas Lights & Independence Day, both cars are in operation and they run in convoy-mode a quarter of a mile apart and within sight of each other. The motormen carry radios and cell-phones to keep in contact, since there is one siding near the centre of the line and that is used for the cars meeting and passing. In these cases, 813 will take the siding, as 48 has a tendency to de-rail if it tries to enter it. However the majority of the passengers prefer to ride on 48, especially on the top deck "as it is more fun". On an average year Standard 48 will travel about 3,200 miles - 132 round-trips over the line - while Brill 813 averages over 4,000 miles. Certainly the continued operation of 48 needs consideration owing to high maintenance costs, but this has been a considerable achievement for a Blackpool tram, after 37 years successfully operating in the U.S.A.! *(Congratulations and thanks to Roy E. Bonn, retired General Manager of Willamette Shore Trolley)*

Standard 147 – Too Tall for Trolleyville!

The most remarkable of all the Blackpool trams that made the journey to U.S.A. must be 147, the one that has returned to stay. Following the examples of 144 and 48 operating in American Museums, Trolleyville's founder - Gerald E. Brookins - offered to purchase 147 for service on his private line at Olmstead Falls in Cleveland, Ohio. 147 was last used in passenger service during 1966 Season at Blackpool. After a farewell Standard Car tour for enthusiasts on 29th October l966, 147 was shipped in September 1967 to the Port of Cleveland via St. Lawrence Seaway and Lake Erie. Upon arrival, it was found that its height of 17ft 6ins made the car touch Trolleyville's overhead, and thus precluded its operation. At that time, unfortunately it stood in the open against the severe elements during two snowy winters, until a compact shed was constructed to protect the car. 147 was hidden there for thirteen years, when it became possible to transfer it to a barn, where the museum kept its running fleet. Some initial and limited restoration work was carried out, which involved the ruby quarter-lights being removed from one side and the top deck being partially painted. Then work ceased and 147 was returned to a barn where the "demic" cars were kept. It had been long felt in Blackpool that 147's return would be desirable, but finally a formal approach was made in 1999. Blackpool Transport found that Trolleyville was prepared to part with 147, providing that it was exchanged for a more suitable Blackpool tram. Examples of Boat-cars in Philadelphia and San Francisco showed that a Boat at Trolleyville would be attractive to visitors. 147 remained in the barn until late September, when she emerged into the light of day once more, to be made ready for her journey back to Blackpool. A team from Blackpool carried out extensive preparatory work, including bracing the top deck to ensure the deck-splitting would be successful. On Monday 2nd October, everything proceeded according to plan and the two separate saloons were loaded for transportation to Baltimore and onward to Seaforth. 147 was welcomed to Blackpool in a downpour on Monday 23rd October, when it was immediately re-assembled and towed into the depot, 33 years and 47 days after it departed! Thus this story boasts an ideal conclusion. The refurbishment process of 147 is progressing well, at the time of writing. The return of 147 to her native rails in regular service is anticipated at Easter 2002, and this is eagerly awaited!

147 at Trolleyville in October 2000, prior to its departure for Blackpool again. Notice the bracket-arm height and the overhead close to the roof. **Graham Twidale**

Celebrate in Philadelphia by Boat 603

A historic setting in Philadelphia for Boat 603, carrying passengers on route 50 along 5th Street. Notice the folding step to the higher platform, the wider wheels and "Pittsburgh Paints" on the indicator. Clearly this has been the source of its colourful appearance!
Ian M. Dougill

BLACKPOOL BOAT 603 HELPS PHILADELPHIA CELEBRATE THE BICENTENNIAL!

In 1976, when Blackpool Borough celebrated its Centenary, it acquired the Dreadnought from the National Tramway Museum, and simultaneously the U.S.A. was celebrating its Bicentennial, in Philadelphia where they requested Blackpool to loan them a Boat-car. It was agreed that Boat 603 would be on-hire to SEPTA in Philadelphia, and the charge was to be a silver-dollar for 1976 and an advance of 75-cents for 1977! Thus 603 left Blackpool on 6th February 1976, and arrived in Philadelphia early in March. After re-gauging it to 5 foot 3 inches for their system, 603 was raised on its mounting, so that the bogies would clear the side panels when turning curves. Since its platform was then higher off the ground, 603 was fitted with a pneumatically-operated platform step, and was finished in a striking white and orange livery, complete with sweeping three coloured flares. Along with several other vintage cars borrowed from museums, 603 entered a special Bicentennial service on 2nd August. This ran along the historic single track on 4th and 5th Streets, between Girard Avenue and Catherine Street, and the 35 cent fare was charged. Blackpool Boat-car 603 was hoped to operate for three seasons, with its possible loan to New Orleans in the winter. Unfortunately, this move within the U.S.A. did not happen, and 603 spent the winter in Luzerne depot. In 1977, during the summer months on Saturdays, Boat 603 was on route 15 between 60th Street and Cumberland Avenue, using normal fares. There was the novelty of riding through the under-pass in the open air and gave the passengers an unusual experience! On 12th July 1978, 603 returned to Blackpool on board the "Atlantic Conveyor", via the Royal Seaforth Container Terminal. Since it remained in the Philadelphia livery, 603 was not used again in Blackpool until San Francisco asked for it in 1985 and she returned to the U.S.A., becoming our most travelled tram!

A Trio of Blackpool's Boats – Now in the U.S.A.

In 2001, sixty-seven years since twelve Boat cars were a novel introduction to the Blackpool tramway system, five remain here and three have emigrated to the U.S.A., in different locations. While four of the Boats were scrapped in 1968, following the reduction of the system by the loss of the street routes and Marton depot, the first Boat 601 sailed over the Atlantic. Since in Autumn 1971, there was a British Trade Fair to take place in San Francisco, the California Railway Museum subsequently bought this Boat at a nominal-sum. Initially the intention was to operate 601 on the MUNI city-system to advertise the forthcoming Trade Fair. It is certain that details of the bogies - like the wheel profile and gauge - were sent to MUNI before it arrived. 601 was withdrawn prior to leaving on the 19th August for Liverpool, before which publicity photographs were taken by the Central Information Office. The use of this unusual open tram was planned to operate along the famous Market Street, amongst the PCC trams of the system. Unfortunately, this was thwarted by a prolonged dock strike there. Hence its vessel "MS Sinaboa" arrived off San Francisco on 7th October, from which Boat 601 could not be unloaded directly on to the Bay Area Electric Railroad, until October 13th. Then - having missed the British Trade Fair - it was transferred to California Railway Museum at Rio Vista Junction. In retrospect it seemed a mistake, but its subsequent operation in San Francisco 1983-85 made its transfer to the U.S.A. worthwhile!

A picturesque scene of 226 at Rio Vista Junction Railway Museum, with passengers waiting for a long ride.   **Ian M. Dougill**

California
Railway
Museum

Boat 226 travelling through the wheat-fields of California, and about to make a return-trip from here. It shows the correct livery with its elegant tower, and even two Blackpool crests on the doors!
Ian M. Dougill

In 1983, with the closure of the famous Cable Car System in San Francisco for restoration, it was decided to create a Trolley Car Festival along the Market Street line, which had just been replaced by a new subway-line for the service routes. Thus it was intended to operate twelve museum cars on the F-line from the East Bay Terminal to Castro, during May to September. While using some of MUNI vintage trams, it was necessary to borrow other trams from museums, in order to create the interest and patronage of the tourists. Clearly the two California Museums, at Rio Vista and Glenwood were approached, and from the former came Blackpool Boat 601. By this time it had been repainted in the correct original livery, with its number 226. Whilst at the museum it had a trolley-tower, which had to be removed for the lower overhead in San Francisco, and was fitted with a mini-tower to carry the trolley. Amongst the variety of foreign cars to be seen along Market Street, then included Blackpool 226, Melbourne 648, Hamburg 3557 and two from Oporto. By December, the fine weather had contributed to the success of the Trolley Festival, and made Blackpool 226 the most popular car! During the 1984 Season, 226 continued in operation, and was still used in December when the weather was fine. While the reopening of the Cable Car Lines began again in June, this reduced the loading on the Trolley Festival cars, although they were well patronised by locals! MUNI had established that Blackpool Boat-car 226 had been very useful, and while its place was in the Museum at Rio Vista, it would be sensible to acquire their own Boat-car from Blackpool. It was known about a disused Boat 603, which had been previously loaned to Philadelphia in 1976 for the Bi-Centennial, and was still in the orange & white livery. An approach was made, and Blackpool with their forthcoming Centenary in 1985, was pleased to meet the needs of San Francisco. Thus Boat 603 - to be renumbered 228 - left Blackpool on 19th February and became the most travelled Blackpool tram in its history! The Trolley Festival finished on 15th October 1985 and while Boat 226 returned to its Museum at Rio Vista, two Blackpool Boat-cars were coincidentally present in 1985.

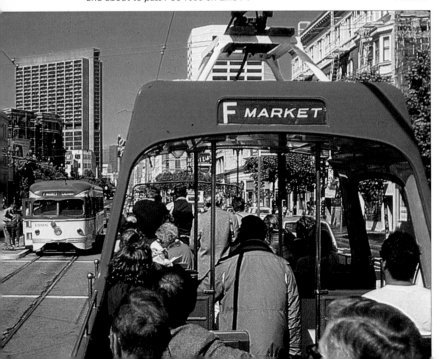

In 1986 at the California Mint, Boat 228 looks attractive, showing "50th Anniversary of the Bay Bridge", and still flying the Union Jack! **Author**

Riding down Market Street on 228, which is popular in good weather, and about to pass PCC 1006 on Line F . **Author**

San Fransisco Trolley Festival Boat 228

When I visited San Francisco in August 1986, it gave me the greatest pleasure to see Boat 228 operating in the busy traffic of Market Street. Along with the street-cars of many types, it proved to be popular for an open ride on a sunny day, for suited businessmen as well as sightseeing tourists. I found that it had been fitted with 48 new wooden seats by MUNI, reduced in order to provide more room for the younger generations in the U.S.A.. Suffice to say, its original seats had been removed by Blackpool in 1985 for use in the open-top of 706, and thus San Francisco had received some surplus ones. A trolley-retriever had been mounted on the inside dash at each end, and a signal bell had been mounted on the platform, instead of the electric bell. While 228 was in its traditional Blackpool livery, its sides commemorated "50 Years of the Bay Bridge", in a striking profile. At that time 228 was single ended, because only one of the three acquired BTH B-18 controllers was effective! MUNI-Engineer - Karl Johnson - told me that 228 had struggled up the incline on Market Street towards Duboce Avenue, but a 600-volt system did help it! Undoubtedly the sight of Boat 228 was enhanced by the flying of the Union Jack and the Stars & Stripes flags from each corner-post, while the Skull and Crossbones was mounted at the top of the trolley-rope. Perhaps the driver should have looked like the Pirate King in this situation! However, this confirmed the original popularity of Boats in Blackpool, especially when they operated Circular Tours, and now likewise in the U.S.A..

Fisherman's Wharf F-Line

At Pier 39 of Fisherman's Wharf, with Boat 228 and Streetcar 1, on the day that the Mayor of San Francisco opened the new line - 21st March 2000. **Author**

"Ride a Muni F-Line vintage street-car down Embarcadero to Fisherman's Wharf, and catch a front-row seat on one of the historic street-cars that come out for special occasions - like a popular open-top Boat-car 228 from Blackpool in England."

Certainly this created my excuse to visit San Francisco once more, and thus I was there on 21st March, when the Mayor launched the new line to Fisherman's Wharf with a procession of historic cars, including Boat-car 228, Melbourne 496, Milan Peter-Witt 1834 and 1914 Muni B-type 130. The purpose of the new Embarcadero line provided access to Fisherman's Wharf for the tourists from Market Street, as an alternative to the popular cable-cars, which have long queues formed and delays in boarding them during the day. Now the Market Street line has been restored to the traditional Ferry Building, where a new attractive Plaza has been created. The street-cars now run along the Embarcadero on a reservation, which is lined by giant palm trees and gives a splendid view of the Bay together with the restored and imposing Harbour buildings. When the street-car line reaches Fisherman's Wharf at Pier 39, it becomes a single line along the Promenade, lined by boutiques, amusement arcades and restaurants, turning into Jones Street as the terminus. In the afternoon of that special day, I stood at Pier 39 watching the colourful PCCs passing, and then surprisingly, Boat 228 appeared round the corner with its flags flying in the wind! This location proved appropriate for a coastal tramway and therefore popular with the passengers, viewing the picturesque bay with its famous former prison Alcatraz. The Boat-car then returned along Beach Street performing a Shuttle service, and I rode it for a journey to the Ferry Building. Incidentally, one of the local passengers said she thought that 228 came from Australia, and then found it was from England!

When I visited the depot at Balboa Park, I was told that the Boat-car was not possible to be used on the complete F-line from Castro to Fisherman's Wharf, because of regulations requiring boarding facilities by disabled people. These had to be fulfilled by each street-car and every stop has now been provided with a ramp for wheelchairs. All PCC cars carry a folding metal-bridge, but that is not possible by the Boat-car with a low centre platform. The Engineer - Karl Johnson - informed me that there would have to be a modification of 228, possibly by widening the driver's door at each side to admit a wheelchair. When this is completed, Boat 228 would be seen more frequently on Market Street, as I previously saw it there in 1986. On this occasion - in March 2000 - it was pleasing to see this Blackpool tram looking very smart, having been repainted recently and released from the canvas tent which covered it during the winter months. In the Muni Historic-fleet for fifteen years, 228 has undoubtedly proved its success as an attraction, especially during good weather!

A TOUR OF SAN FRANCISCO - BY STREET-CARS 1 & 228 - MARCH 2000

One of the first happy experiences during my visit to San Francisco was seeing it again by a tour on Muni 1 and Boat 228. The U.K. party boarded the cars at 11th Street - a spur off Market Street - and the journey towards the Ferry Building provided us with an unusual view of the tall buildings, alternating between sunshine and the cold shadows of March. Passing us were service PCCs, painted in a variety of colours representing former city-fleets, giving them names like "Bumble Bee" of Cincinatti, "Green Harvest" of Chicago, "Cream Cheese" of Philadelphia. As we turned left to travel along the Embarcadero, amusingly the Boat's indicator was showing "PLEASURE BEACH via PROMENADE". What a pity we have not got an American PCC at Blackpool, to represent San Francisco! Having returned along Market Street, we then toured the suburban routes starting with J-Line Church, involving climbing through the open park at Mission Dolores, and looking back at the city landscape. We then progressed to Balboa Park and passed the tramway depots, but Boat 228 had a struggle climbing the hill towards Ingleside, and thus the passengers had to disembark until it achieved success. Actually it ran short of sand for its wheels gripping the rail, and we could have brought some sand-bags with us from Blackpool! We travelled along the reservation toward the entrance of the Twin Peaks Tunnel, but we turned left towards Taraval on the L-line. A short-working involved us returning to Ocean View, but Muni-1 was left behind by Boat 228, and did not join it until we reached Market Street. Its passengers claimed that it was exceeding 40 mph downhill, and had been "clocked" by a motorist who told them! Certainly this had been a memorable occasion for all the British enthusiasts, especially those - like the author - from native Blackpool.

In March 2000, the weather was fine for tour on Boat 228 and MUNI-1, seen here at Ferry Square, along with PCC in Los Angeles livery. **Graham Weaver**

228 approaches the stop with "Any Time" showing on the sign. **Graham Weaver**

Boat 606 Transfers to Trolleyville

A nostalgic scene on 21 August 2000 showing 606, North Euston Hotel and the Lighthouse, on its last authentic visit to Fleetwood on a Market Day - never to be seen again!
Author

After a long journey from Blackpool, 606 arrives at Trolleyville in exchange for Standard 147.
Mike Airey

In the Nineties – Centenary Preparations!

Undoubtedly the Blackpool Tramway, complete with restored historic trams, must always look interesting in order to attract the tourists and the tram enthusiasts alike. Since the Centenary of the Promenade Tramway in 1985 was celebrated by a procession of twenty trams from several cities, and included historic Blackpool trams: Conduit-car 4, Dreadnought 59 and Standard 40. Therefore the Centenary of the Blackpool & Fleetwood Tramroad in 1998 had to be correctly celebrated in this tradition. At the opening of the decade in 1990, Dreadnought 59 was still present, after fourteen years since the Borough Centenary in 1976, but was reclaimed by the National Tramway Museum at the end of that Season. The Dreadnought performed its last tour over the whole system on 11th November, with a special stop at the Foxhall, where the ancient public house was being demolished. It was rather sad that 59 left its native resort, where it had become popular with tourists, providing rides on the open top-deck! Looking back at those original years 1902-1934, Dreadnoughts were ideal with their wide steps at each end, thus able to load and unload simultaneously. Since 59 had been retained in Copse Road Depot after 1934, from which it was resurrected in 1960 to celebrate the 75th Anniversary of the Promenade Tramway. Upon its return to Crich in 1990, it was hoped that it would be in popular usage there, but sadly it has remained for ten years in the Clay Cross store, narrowly missing the fire which took place there in 1999. Since it will be a hundred years old in 2002, there must be an opportunity to see it again, at Crich or in Blackpool.

The two vintage trams Dreadnought 59 and Box 40 taking part in the 1990 F.T.S. Convention, and seen crossing over at the Pleasure Beach in their final year together.
Author

The charming sight of newly repainted Bolton 66 passing parked vintage buses in North Albert Street on the 1989 Fleetwood Tram Sunday.
Author

More relevant to the 1998 Centenary was the presence of Tramroad Box 40, which had been restored at Heaton Park - including fitting new wheel-tyres, repanelling the sides, rewiring and repainting it there. 40 arrived on Tuesday 14th June 1988, and had been sponsored by Fisherman's Friend, who had paid for its restoration and thus claimed its advertisements in return. While contrasting in style, 40 and 59 were seen together for three years on tours, and finally after 40's solo year in 1991, the National Tramway Museum claimed its return there. There was a final tour on 3rd November, when it was nearly trapped in Fleetwood by a large articulated wagon which had stalled across the tram track in North Albert Street. Then in an unique reverse tour through the Ferry to the North Albert Street crossover, finally enabled 40 return to the depot. After a season of display in the Crich Exhibition Hall, it joined Dreadnought 59 in Clay Cross store. The loss of such historic trams deprived Blackpool of attraction and interest in the tramway, and thus forward planning became necessary for the future success of the 1998 Tramroad Centenary.

However the Tram Sunday of 1991 continued to maintain a fine tradition, first established in 1985, and the procession of trams was led by Box 40, and followed by Bolton 66, Princess Alice 706, Boat 605 and Vanguard 619. Of course this event was becoming more popular, as the crowds grew greater each year, and the display of vintage buses, cars and commercial vehicles was enhanced by the service of vintage trams. This provided an excellent viewing of the exhibits between the Ferry and Ash Street, travelling at slow speeds. Each year, the Fleetwood Tram Sunday Committee has succeeded in improving the Transport Festival by adding the traction engines, carousel roundabouts, brass bands, and interesting stalls - with transport books, pictures and souvenirs. Fleetwood has proved to be the unique British town - with a tramway serving its streets - thus becoming the perfect location for a Tram Sunday! The historic trams which appear on this occasion provide the "icing on the cake", and have achieved success each year, until their disappearance in 2000, owing to the transport workers' strike. Even without the trams, "Tramless Sunday" remained successful.

During the Nineties, Blackpool achieved success in repainting some of its trams in colourful liveries, creating a striking image amongst the service-cars. In the first place was the restoration of Boat 605 in its traditional livery, and sponsored by the Fylde Tramway Society. Boat cars 602 & 604 were given different liveries of notable buses at that time: 602 being in the yellow-and-black of the Handy Buses, while 604 was in the red-and-white of the traditional London Routemasters used on the Promenade bus service. On 17th February 1991, Balloon 701 having been rebuilt, was also given the red and white livery, complete with lining in black and white. It did catch the eye along the Promenade, and thus was ideal for advertising Blackpool Transport Travel Cards. Amongst the service-cars, Brush car 636 had been repainted in a Wartime style in 1989, commemorating the outbreak of the 2nd World War fifty years ago. In 1991, car 5 one of the remaining OMOs - appeared in a most attractive style with green roof and skirt around the panels, which was first inaugurated on Centenary car 646. This proved to be the OMO finale, followed by their withdrawal early in 1993.

In 1996 with the Centenary approaching, Blackpool Transport had opened discussions with the National Tramway Museum, for the loaning of those trams which would depict the evolution of the Blackpool & Fleetwood Tramroad. Clearly the two Company cars, 1898 Crossbench-car 2 and 1914 Box 40 saloon were essential for the occasion, together with Pantograph 167 of 1928. Incidentally, it was deemed that a refurbished Vanguard 619 would have to be substituted for the 1898 car, if 2 was not to be allowed to return here again. The first successful acquisition in 1996 was Box 40, which had been stored in Clay Cross and was therefore disused at the Museum. In order to raise the cost of transportation and its repainting, "Friends of 40" guaranteed its return on 22nd April. The unusual sight of 40 travelling along the M55 - on a low-loader - enabled your author to provide leadership back to the depot. As it progressed along the former tram route of Lytham Road, people stood at the bus stops and recognised it as a familiar sight. Once it rolled down the rail-ramp of the transporter, 40 was pushed by Brush car 631 into the compound of the depot, next to Bolton 66.

A colourful scene at the Ferry, with OMO 5 and Boats 604 & 602 in May 1990. **Author**

At the Cabin as Brush-car 636 in wartime livery passes OMO 5 in a new style fleet livery. **Author**

Box 40 returns home again in the early evening. **Author**

In the Paint Shop lettering on the display board of 40 is taking place in July 1998. **Author**

In order to restore its safe operation, new head and tail-lights were fitted beneath the main frame at each end, and a long trolley complete with rope was installed. While this was not the original short trolley - set at a steep angle, it was felt better to avoid dewirements on the re-fitted overhead. In order to thank Fleetwood Tram Sunday Committee for their financial support, on Monday 6th June, 40 was driven to Bold Street outside the North Euston Hotel, where Chairman Jim Cowpe presented a cheque to cover the cost of its repainting. A short journey then took place through the town centre to Fisherman's Walk, as a nostalgic ride for the Committee members, following which it made its lively way back to the depot, still advertising "FISHERMAN'S FRIEND". Thus it was back where it should be, on a ten year loan, and work soon began upon a full repainting in time for Fleetwood Tram Sunday. In the paint shop, rubbing-down of the well worn external body surfaces, and the interior saloon took place, and it was soon restored into its striking chestnut brown and cream livery, with gold lining. In addition, the expert sign-writers applied the large gold lettering - " BLACKPOOL & FLEETWOOD ELECTRIC TRAMROAD" to the lower-panel, with the upper display-board announcing the " BLACKPOOL & FLEETWOOD TRAMROAD CENTENARY 1898 - 1998", sponsored by the "Tram Sunday Committee and the North Euston Hotel". However, it was strange that the semi-circular "BLACKPOOL & FLEETWOOD" was missing from the end-dash panels. This undoubtedly was to avoid confusion for the passengers with the destination shown on the refitted indicator-box, dating from the Corporation era of the Twenties. The commercial situations on a tramway would always decide on the ideal, even for a historic tram like 40!

On 21st July, the 12th Fleetwood Tram Sunday became a special occasion, since the procession of trams was led by the newly repainted Box 40. However it came at a great surprise to find that it was followed by Balloon 719, dressed as the Walls Ice Cream parlour for serving the product on-board, and the open-top Stockport 5. Following its restoration at Mode Wheel in Salford, 5 had arrived in Blackpool on 28th May, and was handed over to Blackpool Transport by its owner Stan Heaton on 11th June. The height of its upper deck panels had been raised to secure passenger safety, and because of the financial support of the Pleasure Beach showed its advertisement. On this first occasion when it appeared on Tram Sunday, it was shown purely to give a ride to the working party who had ensured its delivery! After resting at the Ferry loop, so that its resistances could cool down with its trolley lifted from the overhead, it then returned to Blackpool at the end of the morning. Since the Railway Inspectorate would need to approve such a new type for the tram fleet, air-brakes would be fitted before it went into general service. Although this car did not relate to the Centenary, it joined Bolton 66 which had first arrived in 1981, and had been found useful for Promenade usage and hiring. Certainly an open-topper was a popular tram by the Seaside, as previously was the Dreadnought and also Balloon 706. However, since 5 was fitted with a four-wheel truck from Oporto, she gave a somewhat bouncing ride on the reserved track, and would have been better on the Promenade!

At the new Fisherman's Walk clock tower, Stockport 5 has arrived for the first time for the 1996 Tram Sunday, behind Walls Ice Cream 719.
R.P. Fergusson

700 Restored as a "Green Balloon"

Boat 605 & Balloon 700 are seen together in rather striking wartime livery at the Pleasure Beach.
Terry Daniel

RETURN OF MARTON 31 & BOAT 600

In planning for the Centenary it had been necessary to consider a procession showing the full range of trams over the history of the Blackpool and Fleetwood line. Since the double-deckers were first introduced to Fleetwood on 1st June 1958, and the first one from North Station was in the traditional green livery with twin indicators. Consequently, a decision was made that the first of the Balloons - 700 originally numbered 237 - should be restored to permanently represent that chapter in its history. Thus early in 1996, 700 was stripped down to its body frame, removing the front of the driver's cabs. It was first fitted with a strengthened main frame and then was repanelled in the Body Shop during August. The most notable features to be restored were the twin indicators and opening windscreens at each end, along with the half-drop windows in the saloons. These would be complete with glass louvres and mock ventilators above them on the exterior. In the saloons, the restoration of the Alhambrinal ceilings had not been possible and had to be replaced by fibreglass panelling lined by varnished teak wood frames. Similarly, the distinctive patterned linoleum was - in terms of safety - replaced by beige coloured anti-slip covering. Appropriate was that the centre indicator-box over the door was restored and permanently showing "PROMENADE". The original metal numbers - 237 - were fixed in the traditional position over the centre doors. Within the driver's cabs, the chrome surface of the E.E. Z6 controllers and the wheels of the hand-brake were restored. For the passengers, the customary reversible seats were installed in the upper and lower saloons, re-covered with moquette. However, to establish its enclosure in 1942, the original padded wooden seats should have been retained in the upper saloon. 700 appeared at Easter 1997 fitted with the appropriate trolley, and first visited Fleetwood on Easter Sunday, attracting the attention of the public, since it looked smart and compared more favourably with the other Balloons in service.

During 1997, the plans to achieve success with the Centenary included the importance of identifying the dates. Clearly 1st July was the most important, since in 1898 there took place the inaugural journey of Crossbench-car 4 to Fleetwood. Consequently it would be important to borrow Crossbench-car 2 from the National Tramway Museum, but it seemed that its limited use would be confined to this, along with the Depot Open Day on 28th June and a "Grand Cavalcade" on July 12th. There was considerable reluctance to allow Crossbench-car 2 - with it running boards to facilitate easy access - to be used on Tram Sunday, owing to the crowded location of the Fleetwood streets and possible accidents. However in history, the provision of folding running-boards on the Llandudno toastracks did enable them to be safer whilst in motion. If this example was applied to No. 2, it would have enabled it to be safely operated here! Certainly, the Fleetwood Tram Sunday Committee felt that at least that No. 2 could arrive at the head of the procession and be displayed during the day, perhaps at the Ferry! Pantograph 167, which in 1985 had been loaned for the season, again had been requested from April until November, and the loan of Boat 605 being offered in return. Subsequently this was not accepted, and l67 made a minimal stay for the Centenary events, along with Crossbench car 2. Prior to their delivery in 2000, complete restoration of 2 took place during the previous winter, and Pantograph 167 was completely repainted, ready for returning to Blackpool.

Behind the scenes in the Workshop at Crich, the two cars are seen in final preparation for the Centenary in Blackpool - June 1998.   **Author**

The newly arrived Marton 31 in the yard at Rigby Road, is being released on to its native rails.
Author

Much more successful negotiation for borrowing Marton Box car 31 became a reality, when it arrived from Beamish North East Open Air Museum on the l0th September. In this case, Blackpool had retained ownership when it was released for restoration on 17th July 1984. Certainly it was magnificently restored and was inaugurated at the Museum on 17th August 1988, when it became a great asset. During its return to Blackpool for twelve months, it had been agreed that 31 would be fitted with new tyres on the wheels of the Preston bogies and repainted during the winter months of 1997, ready for the Centenary year. However it was rewarding when it was seen in action during the 1997 Illuminations. On 3rd December, to complete the historic cars, Boat 600 arrived from Heaton Park, where it had been on loan in exchange for Manchester 765, in 1985. Fortunately, it proved to be in good condition, and this would facilitate its restoration for the 1998 Centenary celebrations. The family of Boats was thus restored to six in Blackpool, and there were a further two - 601 and 603 - in California! All was ready here - for 1998.

A delightful scene at Fleetwood in the evening sun, with 31 turning towards the Ferry in July 1998.
Terry Daniel

The Fascinating Season of 1998

To commence the significant year of 1998, Friends of 40 hired this tram on January 3rd for a ride along the coast to Fleetwood and enjoy a lunch in the historic North Euston Hotel. However, we were warned that the weather was ominous, with the tide becoming rough and thus 40 was in spray as it journeyed along South Promenade. While turning on the loop at Starr Gate, all the lights of 40 went out and the car became static, because the trolley had been blown off. It was clear that its rope was dangling on the other side of a tall fence, and much to everyone's amusement, the driver climbed the fence and passed the rope to his conductor. He then resumed the tour, driving 40 quickly away from South Shore. Arriving at North Pier, 40 was greeted by Marton-car 31, which was being filmed by a television drama team, in a storm. Once we were on the traditional reservation north of the Cabin, we had an elevated position with a dramatic coastal view of the raging sea. However, when travelling through Rossall farming-fields we were reminded of the original Tramroad-line, which that year would reach its Centenary and be celebrated. When 40 arrived at Fleetwood Ferry, the height of the tide was such that it lapped at the edge of the Promenade, and we were warned not to leave before the high-tide at 1400. During the lunch in the Vantini Room NEH, we were able to reflect upon the forthcoming year of the Centenary, and the immense effort which would be needed to raise funds for the return of the historic trams Crossbench-car 2 and Pantograph-car 167. Together, along with restored Box 40, they would illustrate the fleet development in the first thirty years of the Tramroad. Also your author did forecast the production of his book "Blackpool & Fleetwood 100 Years By Tram" by July 1st! Our journey back to the depot was unexpectedly terminated at North Pier, since Central Promenade had been closed by tidal obstructions. A Handy Bus was provided and 40 remained a nostalgic sight, looking handsome in its restored livery and shining with its lights. In retrospect, this occasion would have warned us about the gale-force day of the Centenary procession in July. Indeed North Pier had also lost its jetty on that day, which was never restored!

The Cleveleys Square active scene in January 1998, as Centenary 647 travels on the new track, with the unfinished north-bound track in the foreground.
Author

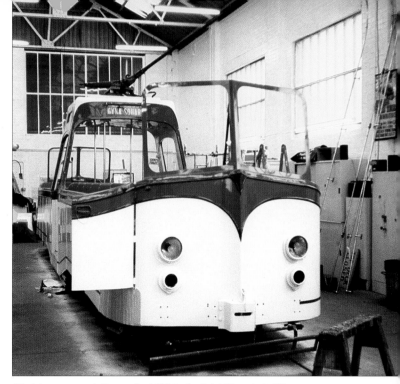

A contrast between rebuilt Balloon 707 and Trampower 611 in the depot compound. **Author**

Work is near completion on Boat 600 in the Paint Shop, but still without a trolley tower. **James Millington**

Thinking of the early period of the Centenary Year, it was pleasing to reflect upon the track relaying in Cleveleys Square, with a single line service cars working to and from Little Bispham. This did provide a novelty for the tram passengers, circling the loop to regain the correct track again. Of course they had never previously experienced it themselves - unless they had been on a Circular Tour. Down at Rigby Road depot, scenes of unusual trams did provide an interest for the tramway enthusiasts. The long-time missing Boat-car 600 had returned from Manchester Heaton Park on 3rd December 1997, and was taken into the Body-shop where inspection did find that it was in good condition. Thus it was to retain its original panelling of 1934, however its later plastic windscreen was replaced with more modern glass windscreens, being taller to compensate for the lower sides. 600 had taken the place of Balloon 707 in the Body -shop, which had been rebuilt in a new style and was repainted by January. Work to 707 continued in the depot compound, on the wiring of the new air-conditioning in the driver cabs. While 707 looked quite striking in appearance, the fault lay in the appearance of the front upper-deck window and the similar sized indicator panel immediately beneath it. General comments were made that the lower-deck front appearance looked smart, although unfortunately it was without the driver cab doors. Undoubtedly the general upper-deck appearance at each end needed a more stylish appearance. When one thinks of the Art Deco style of the Balloons, they are still of attractive appearance to this day, and are worthwhile keeping! After more than 65 years in-service, cars like 707 must demonstrate new and effective style, which would be beneficial to both the passengers and the crew. The best previous example is Jubilee car 762, which was rebuilt with a front entrance and centre exit, and thus has only required a single-crew in the winter plus one conductor in summer. One hopes that such previous experience ensures better development in the future, since the air-conditioning proved to be unpopular with the drivers of 707 and 709, and was subsequently replaced by opening windows - for fresh air!

Of more stimulus at that time was the presence in the depot-compound of the new Roadliner articulated car, with work upon its electrical wiring taking place. My discussion with the leader of the Pullman team, led me to understand that trials would be made on the system, first regarding its clearances on curved track leading into the depot. This would be followed round the curves of the system, for the approval of the Railway Inspectorate and followed by the drivers' training. Then it might have been possible for the use of the interesting Roadliner - being able to carry 200 passengers - for the public. Undoubtedly there were two aspects here: the use of such a long car and with five doors into the three-section saloon. This was at the lower-level than all the other conventional trams here, and thus the public would have found it easier to board and leave, than on the higher platforms of the others. Blackpool Transport would have found a larger-capacity tram useful on the Promenade, where there is busy loading in the Season. This would surpass the sixty year-old railcoaches which have only a 48-seat capacity, and need a crew of two. Interestingly, the Pullman demonstrator was a British creation at a lesser-cost - circa £750,000 - and thus cheaper than the Continental types used in Manchester, Sheffield, Birmingham and Croydon. In that year, the coincidence of the Tramroad Centenary showed a requirement for the future development of the fleet. The success of the Roadliner here would have ensured its future success, on prospective systems to be created in the U.K..

The month of February 1998 saw another visit of SPENO from Switzerland, with the intention of improving the noisy corrugations of the Promenade track between Gynn Square and Cocker Street. This had not been dealt with during a previous visit in 1995, but a repeat action took place on the street tracks of Fleetwood Lord Street and the Metropole. It seemed at that time a great pity that the noisy road crossing between Copse Road and Radcliffe Road in Fleetwood was neglected, despite that it also needed renewing. It is understood that SPENO subsequently visited other tramways in Britain and while it proved costly, it did surpass the traditional grinder 752 here. On March 31st there was a surprise with the arrival of Glasgow Coronation 1245 from the East Anglia Transport Museum, for storage here. This was ironic coincidence between 1245 and the presence of Glasgow Cunarder 1297 for the Promenade Centenary in 1985. Certainly the depot then contained a variety of tram types from a variety of former systems, in Bolton, Stockport and Glasgow, together with Pullman Roadliner from Cardiff!

A white articulated car always needs keeping clean during its trials in April 1998.
Author

March saw the appearance of Boat 600 in the depot, newly painted in the style of the Thirties, complete with dark-green lining, stainless steel strips on the fenders and the addition of the Blackpool Corporation garter coat-of-arms to each side. The Fylde Tramway Society badge in the centre of the trolley-tower indicated its generous sponsor. It was notable on April 7th that Roadliner 611 was seen towed by Engineering-car 754 on the Promenade, being tested for clearance between the Depot and Tower. Towards the end of the month, 611 was seen under power in Hopton Road and repeatedly passing through the tram-washer on test. However the first notable appearance of Boat 600 occurred on Sunday 3rd May, when the F.T.S. enjoyed a journey to Fleetwood on 600 & 706, being a sunny day! Since 706 - Princess Alice - had a trolley again, so these two cars followed the tradition of the Thirties. However, 706 still had the short-canopy roof which was fitted in 1985, to protect passengers in wet weather from being splashed by the pantograph. Originally the gantry-arch was tapered in the style of the trolley towers of the single-deck cars, and created the Art-Deco style. While enthusiasts liked the novelty of such open cars, the public were attracted to ride upon them in fine weather. It was certainly a credit to B.T.S. in 1998, that they had now four trams in their original style: 600, 700, 706, and Coronation 660, which certainly added to the attraction of the fleet!

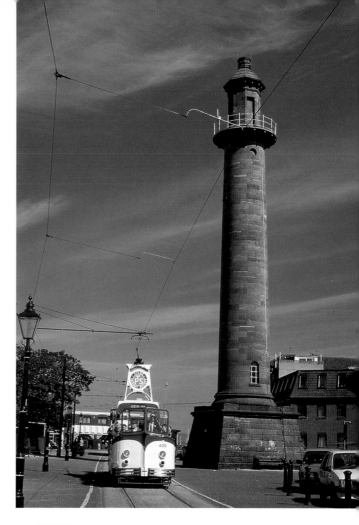

Boat 600 adds to the historic scene in Pharos Street, as it passes the lighthouse.
Author

Showing "COASTAL TOUR" on its indicator, Boat 600 is joined on the siding by open-top 706, making an appropriate seaside scene!
Author

Box 40 turning from Bold Street makes a striking scene, with the North Euston Hotel and a Handy Bus behind **Author**

40 in a traditional Tramroad rural scene with Rossall Farm in the foreground. **Author**

A notable day came on Sunday 17th May, when T.L.R.S. at its Annual Convention hired Box 40 for a journey to Fleetwood. In its traditional location - rather than the Promenade, the attractive repainted body with gold lettering and lining, made a striking appearance. While 40 showed PRIVATE on its indicator, it failed to display the semi-circle of lettering BLACKPOOL & FLEETWOOD traditionally painted beneath its fleet number. However, 40 was enhanced by a new platform door at each end. These had been fitted during the previous winter, following the practice on the Manx Electric Railway cars of the same type. For the Centenary celebrations in July, the actual presence of Crossbench-car 2 would show the traditional lettering on its dash-panels. However, it was felt that this would have been inappropriate, since 40 was fitted with the indicator box dating from the Municipal ownership in the Twenties. Thus, while 40 had the traditional Tramroad Company livery, it has become a car in the commercial fleet of Blackpool Transport, over a period of ten years.

While bound for "STOCKPORT" on the tour, 5 finds this a pleasant location in Fleetwood, with the bowling green in the background.
Author

In the afternoon of the same day, Stockport 5 made only its second journey to Fleetwood since Tram Sunday of 1996, and was hired by its owner Stan Heaton for the enjoyment of its former work force, who had restored it and were now known as "Friends of 5". On such a sunny day, it has always been delightful to ride on an open-top tram, and Dreadnought 59 has been missed since its departure in 1990, for storage at the National Tramway Museum. On Stockport 5 however, passengers should be prepared for the bouncing rhythm of a four-wheel truck, especially on the light rail sleeper track here. Being mounted upon the truck of Oporto 67, its motors are lively in performance and can give a rough ride, when the speed is excessive. Undoubtedly, the striking view of 5's red and white livery with lining, STOCKPORT CORPORATION TRAMWAYS in gold lettering and the Municipal coat of arms, attracted the attention of the public as we passed through Cleveleys Square. When the car arrived at Fleetwood Ferry, there was something of a struggle to gain the siding, as the wheels climbed over the crossing. It necessitated several reversings, as rubber-blocks were inserted against the point-blades to facilitate the fixed-wheels taking them. Once on the siding, the queuing public tried to get on this attractive car but had to be discouraged, while "Friends of 5" took their refreshments in the cafe. The return journey along North Albert Street and Lord Street was very enjoyable, since Stockport 5 was smooth in movement until the reserved track proved lively again, for a 4-wheeler. Subsequently, this car appeared on the Depot Open Day, as a challenge for "pulling the tram". However, it became damaged when its trolley left the overhead and was tangled with the span-wires of the depot fan. This dislodged the trolley-mast from its mounting on the saloon roof, and subsequently it became necessary to fit a steel plate within the roof, for its safety in the future.

Today's Technology for Tomorrow's Tramroad

On the first day of June, Roadliner 611 showed TRAM ON TEST on its indicator, and emerged under its own power, with the Railway Inspector and B.T.S. personnel on board.The first articulated tram in Blackpool set out for Little Bispham loop, and it was seen travelling in surges of speed along the reservation and tentative low speeds over the points and round the loop. The Railway Inspector was observing the body clearance and that it was safe to drive, suffice-to-say very obvious was the car's steady ride and the quiet wheels over the pointwork. The driver was seen to be sat centrally behind the windscreen in an elevated position, thus with good all-round vision. The speed of 611 was achieved by the movement of the "joy-stick" with the driver's right hand, forward-and-back meaning the faster and slower of the speed. The parking brake was the application of a disc-brake on the prop-shaft, which drove the axles by the front-mounted motors. On its return to the depot that Monday afternoon, 611 seemed to leave the service-cars standing, while the elevated Brecknell Willis power-collector looked better than the prominent tower-and-pantograph on the Centenary cars.

An early start was made on the following morning for a travel to Fleetwood, to test 611's performance over the older permanent-way and non-renewed overhead system. Since there would be a more cautious speed in order to enable observation, the first service-car was allowed out before 611 at 5-33 a.m., and the second service-car was allowed to pass 611 at Thornton Gate. The rural scene at Rossall did make the new car very striking in this Centenary Year, and did remind me of the first new Coronation car here in 1952. It was somewhat amusing at Fisherman's Walk, when the tram-signal showed red and did not change, although the traffic lights continued. Consequently the driver of 611 had to reverse it, in order to stimulate the signal in its favour! As the striking Roadliner travelled along Lord Street, it did capture the attention of the local workers, since it undoubtedly looked different from the local trams. As it turned the sharp curves into Bold Street and the Ferry, the mobility of 611's articulations were observed by the Railway Inspector and the staff of B.T.S.. It was distinct that the wheels were very quiet, and then 611 was driven on to the siding so that service-car 648 could pass.

Seen on the trial run approaching Little Bispham on 2nd June.
Terry Daniel

An early morning quiet scene as 611 arrives at Fisherman's Walk.
Author

The return journey was sedate on the northern section of the system, and speeded-up south of Little Bispham to circa-35 mph. The Railway Inspector had every confidence that further trials could take place, followed by the training of tram-drivers operating this K/D system. When this was completed, the Railway Inspector would return to evaluate the use of Roadliner 611 for the carrying of passengers. Of course, this would have been most interesting in the busy Season, and sought to prove its value with a capacity of 200 seated and standing, together with five low-level entrances. Manufacturer Pullman TPL of Cardiff needed several finishing touches to 611, including the lifeguards, signalling-bells, and several saloon facilities for luggage, prams and wheelchairs. Incidentally, the saloon seating and space for standing gave the car an attractive appearance, thus comparing favourably with other older trams here. Undoubtedly this was the great opportunity to prove the value of a new British tram, and created a new generation for Blackpool after more than a hundred years of successful operation. If a class of Roadliners had been adopted here, it would have provided Pullman TPL with the necessary demonstrative publicity. At that time, we hoped that Blackpool would have become the pioneer of a British-built tram again, by the Millennium! Sadly this did not materialise, as problems were found during tests on 611 in 1998-9, concluding that it was removed on August 17th 2000. Its return to Cardiff was for re-appraisal and possible rebuilding. Future developments and success, remain to be seen!

A unique scene at the Ferry, as the service-car passes 611 and the trial team are watching.
Author

On Tuesday 9th June came an unusual sight, as trams were to be seen in Princess Street on trial for the planned Circular Tour on the Blackpool Transport Open Day. Soon after 8 a.m. two VSO vans named TRACK MAINTENANCE, arrived at Foxhall on the Promenade, and the men began cleaning the disused points and the track curve leading across the carriageway. Then ENGINEERING CAR 754 appeared along Blundell Street using its diesel engine, and cautiously made its way round the curve into Princess Street. It was observed passing parked cars in front of the houses, by a policemen and officials of the Borough Surveyors Department, and 754 just managed it! With the Promenade traffic being held up by a BTS official, it was good to see 754 cross the road to join the main-line tramway. Then its trolley was raised for a return journey and was seen, unusually crossing the carriageway and heard rumbling down the little used Princess Street track, with its trolley flickering. Clearly, it would have been better if the track had been cleaned out first, possibly by 752 or a Unimog fitted with brushes. From the open top of 754, observation was made of the trolley-head passing along the recently renewed overhead, complete with new bracket-arms and traction poles. Since all proved satisfactory, 754 returned to the depot and Centenary 646 was used for more trials in this location. When it appeared at the curve from Blundell Street, its length projected it nearer to the curb and thus it was not able to pass the parked cars. An official started knocking at the doors of the nearest houses, in order to ask the owners to remove them from the tram's way. It was thus decided that the tramway curve at this location would have the street marked with keep-clear warning and yellow lattice-marking, to clear its use by trams on the Open Day. Along Princess Street, the Centenary car was pursued by the Unimog wagon, for observation of its pantograph from the tower platform, while one of the staff held it with a trolley-pole. The unusual sight of such a tram in Princess Street and crossing to the Promenade track, showed that the overhead and the points were effective. 646 then returned, with sparks flickering from its pantograph, and all thus seemed clear for the operation of trams along here on the 28th June Open Day. Of course, vintage trams which were planned for use on that occasion, would have trolleys. The 646 trial was useful, for the future use of this route by service cars returning to the depot, while the Hopton Road track was being relaid after the Season. Thus there had been an interesting Tuesday morning in June.

Leaving the Promenade at Princess Street by 754, an unusual sight! **Author**   *Delay in Princess Street as parked cars obstruct Centenary 646.* **Author**

At Crich the crowd watch the appearance of the restored 167 & 2.
James Millington

A delightful scene with 2, 167, 166, and Crich Stand behind them.
Author

On Sunday 21st June, there was a special occasion at Crich for the launching of the two restored Blackpool cars in order for them to return to the seaside for the celebration of the Centenary. There was a large gathering outside the workshop doors, ready to see the two cars emerge together at 1-30 p.m.. When the doors opened, they were driven out together, contrasting in their different fleet liveries and their body styles. 1898 Crossbench 2 carried the original style of oil-lamp in the centre of its chocolate coloured and gold lettered dash panel, while Pantograph 167 showed the Thirties-style body in the Wartime green livery, albeit used in post-war years! The pair of cars from B & F history illustrated the development over thirty years from 1898 to 1928. Speeches were made by T.M.S. President Richard Wiseman, who thanked the work of the painter who had worked l2 hours-a-day to complete 167. Also John Shawcross of the workshop, who said that he would lose some sleep while the two cars were at Blackpool!

Then the two cars made their first journey through Wakebridge to Glory Mine terminus carrying all their supporters, during which I heard the wooden pillars of the Crossbench car creaking, in response to the newly fitted underframe. Also, I was sorry to note that the original amber quarter-lights had been removed and replaced by white ones covered with shaded film. While its appearance looked smart, the display boards along the roof were plain and therefore would have been better not fitted, in order to create its 1898 appearance for the Centenary. On the other hand, 167 was very quiet-running with the wrong motors, instead of the 50 h.p. G.E.C. WT28L ones, which were distinguishable by howling! On this occasion, it was pleasing that the fleet livery was in the correct shades of green, and the platform was correctly finished in the colours of varnished teak and brown panels. Together with red Toastrack 166, the three Blackpool cars provided a striking appearance in rival liveries and styles, until 4 p.m. when 167 was withdrawn to be prepared for the journey home on the following day. Crossbench 2 followed it into the Works at 5 p.m., having added to the enjoyment of the scene. The sunny weather provided a pleasant overture for the forthcoming Centenary event in their native Blackpool!

Return of Restored 2 & 167 to Blackpool

On the following day, word came to Blackpool that Crossbench 2 and Pantograph 167 had left Crich on two low-loaders at 11 a.m. After being seen approaching Blackpool by 5 p.m. on the M55, the two cars travelled along Squires Gate Lane and South Promenade soon after turning into Blundell Street. The Crich working-party lost no time to erect a rail-ramp from the low-loader to the track, using sleepers and lengths of rail from the Clay Cross Store. Crossbench 2, with somebody holding the hand-brake, was gently released on the cable and soon stood in front of the Transport Office once again - after thirty-five years! Pantograph 167 was nearer to the depot, and although being without its trolley tower, looked immaculate and was quickly lowered on to the track. The trolley tower on a trailer was wheeled inside, and then 167 was pulled and pushed by Unimog 440 into the depot electrical compound. Being on track 17, it was familiar territory for this car, especially since Coronation 660 stood waiting in the same location. The low-loaders which had provided their transportation here, then moved from the single track, while Crossbench 2's trolley was raised to the overhead and it was driven speedily along this familiar track and into Hopton Road. Since it seemed appropriate that it should have been driven into its own depot, an offer for Unimog 440 to push it there, was refused. Unfortunately 2 was halted outside, as there was a flash and bang from its controller and mains-switch, which plunged the depot into darkness. Clearly, there must have been a fault with its controller, and so the Unimog finally pushed 2 inside. Thus both the historic cars were in their native depot again, joining 1914 Box 40 for the first time here in 35 years! Sadly, they had been given only a short visit to Blackpool, in order to enhance this historic occasion and illustrate the development of the fleet since 1898. The working party from Crich spent some time in the Depot on the next day, preparing both cars for driver training on Wednesday 24th June.

The arrival in Blackpool of Crossbench-car 2 & Pantograph 167 on a sunny evening, makes a memorable occasion!   **Author**

A contrasting scene in Cleveleys Square as Centenary 645 passes Crossbench-car 2, making a trial journey for driver training.
Author

On this June morning in pouring rain, I heard that 167 had made its trial run to Fleetwood. In the afternoon, car 2 emerged and I first saw it heading north along Queens Promenade, with a trainee-driver at the controls. After thirty-five years, it seemed amazing to myself that such a familiar tram was here again, on its native track! In Cleveleys Square it contrasted with the service trams, and many heads turned to follow its journey northwards. Drivers took it in turn, under the supervision of David Tudor - principal driver instructor at Crich- while John Shawcross held on to the trolley-rope in case it de-wired at any of the overhead frogs. Unlike its previous speedy journey in 1960, on this occasion Crossbench-car 2 was going sedately, as drivers showed a bit of caution for safety. As it entered the Ferry terminus from Bold Street, the trolley did leave the overhead but it was soon driven on to the loop, and posed next to service Centenary car 644 - providing such historical contrast for the first time. When the sun came out, the return journey was more colourful, and pictured the 100-year old tram attractively in the farming location of Rossall, thus recreating the Tramroad days. Certainly it gave me nostalgic memories of that historic tour in June 1960, when Crossbench 2 came to Fleetwood with Dreadnought 59 for the first time. On this occasion forty years later, it showed how a ride along the Tramroad on this Crossbench-car would be popular and safe, since the horizontal-bars on each side could be lowered, thus containing the passengers. Certainly great caution had been expressed in 1998, concerning the safety of this car - especially along the Promenade - but this should not have applied along the reserved track from Cabin to Fleetwood, with the best contemporary example of the Manx Electric Railway, which is still using crossbench-cars safely!

Open Day at the Depot & Works

The occasion on 28th June recalled the last such an event in 1985, but a great novelty on this occasion was a Circular Tour, travelling out via Lytham Road to the Tower and returning via the historic track in Princess Street and Blundell Street. Before the opening-time at 11-30 a.m., I was in the bus garage seeing the interesting stalls being set-up, along with the arrival of the buses, including municipal ones from Bolton and Blackburn, a Ribble PD2, and many others to follow. In front of the depot was the fine sight of the two Tramroad Company cars Crossbench 2 and Box 40, together with Bolton 66, Pantograph 167 and Coronation 660, while behind the fencing could be seen the new Pullman articulated car 611. At 11-30 the Circular Tour started with Marton open-top 31, Boats 600 and 607, and a large queue developed in Hopton Road. A fully loaded 31 set off first for the Tower, and returned to Foxhall where volunteer B.T.S. crew - including Graham Twidale and James Millington - were manning the points and holding the trolley with a pole! 31 lost its trolley several times, and when Boat 600 arrived, there was close scrutiny of its wheels turning the curve very slowly from the Promenade. I went on 31's second journey and much enjoyed the novel experience of diverting from the Promenade at Foxhall and travelling down Princess Street. However, there was a strange sensation on the tram as it turned the corner into Blundell Street, since the second bogie climbed out of the curve. The journey stopped, and an inspector attempted to drive it in reverse back on to the correct track. Engineering staff then arrived with the Unimog 440, and plates were placed under the wheels, thus enabling each to climb over and drop into the track again. On the third journey 31 derailed again, and after much effort by the Engineering staff, it was decided to withdraw it from the Circular Tour and replace it at 1 p.m. with Bolton 66.

Marton 31 on a tour in Blundell Street, with the Tower in the background, and a blank screen!
Author

Open-day at the depot, with splendid line-up of historic trams: 5, 660, 167, 66, 2, 40, 31.
Author

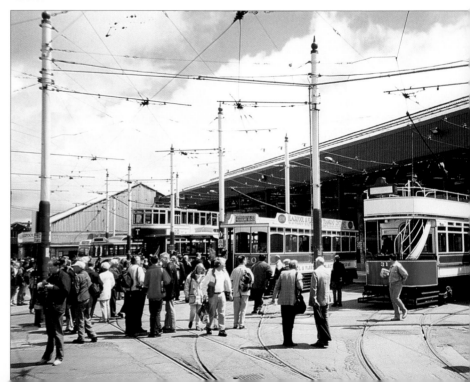

Boat 600 showing RESERVED and cornering from Princess St. to Blundell St., as its wheels are under close observation.
Author

Bolton 66 in Princess Street on the Circular Tour is watched closely by the engineering staff.
Terry Daniel

Fortunately, 66 gave no further problems on the Circular and provided a novel experience for the riders - like myself. There were many other attractions during the afternoon, and there formed a large queue outside the door of the Fitting Shop for a tour of the Works, where it was possible to see the two trams - Balloon 719 and Centenary 642 - stripped down to their framework for rebuilding. In the depot, it was possible to try turning the trolley of Boat 604, and watch the demonstration of the new Roadliner 611 travelling along the empty pit. Then there was a "Pulling the Tram Competition" using Stockport 5, to raise funds for research equipment in the Victoria Hospital. Later unfortunately, it dewired and its trolley caught in the span-wires, which loosened the trolley-mast. Meanwhile, in the bus garage the brass band of a local school echoed from the walls, but it would have been better heard in the yard outside! The finale came with Twin-car 675-685 offering a Circular Tour from Hopton Road, and showing RESERVED on its blind. I rode in the leading-trailer 685, and upon return from the Tower it was unique that the towing-car turned unusually across the road at the Foxhall. There were cries from the duty staff that it had derailed, and it was driven back from the trailer by Inspector Don Penney. The wheels were re-railed and then the Twin-car proceeded along Princess Street followed by a crowd of admirers! At the curve with Blundell Street, the second bogie of the leading car was derailed. Watched by enthusiasts and some residents, the Twin-car was reversed several times until it was able to resume its fascinating journey to the depot. So came the end of the afternoon as the historic trams were shedded, and a large number of in-coming trams queued in Hopton Road. Clearly, good teamwork had been enacted by the BTS volunteer staff that afternoon, and it had proved enjoyable for the enthusiasts and the public present!

Commemoration of 1st Tram to Fleetwood

The recreation of the historic first tram journey on the Tramroad from Blackpool to Fleetwood took place precisely on 1st July 1998. Crossbench 2 and Box 40 arrived at North Pier by 10-45 a.m., but sadly they could not return to the historic location outside North Station. However the BBC North West Tonight team, press and enthusiasts were present. Driven by Graham Twidale, Crossbench car 2 set-off at 11-00 a.m. with a select number of passengers, including the Mayors of Blackpool and The Wyre, and followed by Box 40. Only a few people watched the scene on that sunny day, until we arrived at Bispham, where hundreds of children from the local Primary School were cheering! The historic trams stopped and the Mayors spoke to the crowd, photographs were taken and the BBC filmed it for North West Tonight. At Little Bispham Station, more children were there from the Anchorsholme Primary School waving flags as we arrived, in the tradition of 1898! Certainly this pair of historic Tramroad-cars were ideal to demonstrate for today's school children the original style of riding, on the present tramway. To prepare them for the event, author Steve Palmer had been on a tour of the schools, explaining that 2 & 40 were from the original Tramroad fleet, 2 being 100 years old whereas saloon-car 40 was built in 1914, and hence they contrast in their styles. As we passed through Cleveleys Square, a lot of people stared at the trams and some waved, while the BBC interviewed the passengers on board - those with professional experience and one who has written about it! At Thornton Gate another local school party was waiting, notable for having an annual excursion by tram! Since the BBC wanted to film car 2 from the front, there was manoeuvring of 2's position incorrectly behind 40. The service-car was allowed to pass before 40 led the way with 2 following, and the children gave them a cheer! At Broadwater, children from St. Edmund's Primary School were able to watch the historic trams from the edge of their playing-fields, and the cars slowed down so that the Mayors could greet them.

Thornton Gate with 2 & 40 changing places, are watched by a crowd of local school children.
Ian McLoughlin

A historic sight at Ash Street, with the local children waving to the Mayor of Wyre on board 2. **Author**

Returning along Lord Street, Crossbench-car 2 commemorates the first journey in 1898. **Graham Weaver**

The most notable historic occasion occurred at Ash Street, where hundreds of children from St.Mary's School cheered and waved, just as happened in 1898. For myself, this certainly was a moving occasion, since my grandmother told me how she remembered the first tram - Crossbench 4 - arriving, and as schoolchildren they cheered and waved Union Jacks. So, on this morning we had managed to recreate a memorable scene for Fleetwood. Along Lord Street, some very young nursery children waved as the two trams passed, and finally we arrived at the Ferry. Crossbench-car 2 was parked on the siding, and the official party adjourned to the North Euston Hotel for refreshments. Of course, in 1898 the official party had afternoon-tea at the Mount Hotel and car 4 was parked near London Street, for a crowd of locals to admire. On this occasion, 2 could not halt in Lord Street because of the traffic, and it proved a quieter return journey to Blackpool. Fortunately, the Mayors left at Anchorsholme, since at the road-crossing car 2's controller blew the mains switch and when re-set by the conductor, there was no power in the overhead. Clearly it had blown a switch at the substation at Little Bispham, and thus the service-cars were also halted. The Fleet Engineer contacted the duty-men on the Unimog, and when power was restored and we passed them outside the sub-station, they bowed to respond to the graceful wave of the passengers, including Managing Director Tony Depledge. The driver did decide to drive back slowly, using only series-notches of the controller and avoiding another halt for the service-cars. Certainly this had been a successful occasion for the Centenary, especially involving school children en-route, and consequently helping us to celebrate its survival for 100 years!

Historic Shuttle Service 4th & 11th July

The following Saturday saw the Cleveleys and Fleetwood Heritage tram-shuttle, especially for visiting members of the Tramway Museum Society, using the historic trio. Just before mid-day, Crossbench-car 2 arrived at Bispham full of enthusiastic passengers, and fifteen minutes later Box 40 came, while Pantograph 167 made a familiar appearance by 12-30 p.m.. The sight of 167 recalled working on these cars myself, because Pantographs had been based at Bispham Depot until 1961. Thus they were natives there, since their first appearance in 1928. Whilst their original appearance in red and white livery and a tall pantograph tower was not remembered by present generations, the green livery with the front-flare of post-war years and the trolley-rope certainly were distinctive in our memories! For us on this occasion, 167 made a memorable ride to Fleetwood, by sitting in the saloon with ruby moquette seats, large windows and the red quarter-lights of the clerestory roof. As we passed along Lord Street, the older generation of residents all turned and looked, as such a familiar tram with its distinctive livery was passing again. Undoubtedly, this service with historic cars was every twenty minutes, providing the opportunity for enthusiasts to see these trams in their native Tramroad location - and ride on them! The regular public at tram stops would have welcomed a ride, especially on Crossbench-car 2, but they were prevented from boarding. Later in the afternoon, the vintage cars returned to Bispham for a crew-break and parked on the centre track before returning to Fleetwood, for the early evening.

On the following Saturday 11th July, the same shuttle service started at 8 a.m.for members of the Fylde Tramway Society. The three cars looked very picturesque as they passed each other in the Rossall countryside and the Fleetwood streets. Standing in Albert Square, myself and several enthusiasts were armed with cameras, so that we were able to record the sight of the historic cars passing each other at St. Peter's Parish Church. Unfortunately this lasted only until 12-30 p.m. when the trio was returned to the depot. However, it would have been a valuable opportunity if the ordinary public had been able to sample such interesting trams themselves! This would have been a financial benefit to B.T.S., and essential publicity for the National Tramway Museum at Crich.

Box 40 passing St.Peters Parish Church in Albert Square on its shuttle service, hence showing "PRIVATE" on its indicator.
Terry Daniel

Pantograph 167 was familiar to myself here at Rossall, undoubtedly a scene from the past! **Author**

At Cleveleys Square, the inspector watches the driver - Graham Twidale - pointing out a fault on his historic-car 2. **Author**

Undoubtedly 167 looks very smart in its post-war livery, having been rebuilt in 1936, and is seen here in Bold Street terminus for the shuttle service, and also a view in the saloon. **Author**

Grand Cavalcade of Trams

So came the special event on Sunday 12th July, to commemorate the Centenary for many people, when a cavalcade would leave the Pleasure Beach at 11-00 a.m., led by 1898 Crossbench-car 2. There were many invited guests - including former principal officers, delegates from the tramways of a new generation, and also hundreds of enthusiasts who had booked their seats on a variety of trams in the procession. The appropriate precedent to this occasion was the Promenade Centenary in 1985, when a procession of twenty trams - including those from several cities - attracted a huge crowd on a beautiful sunny day. Unfortunately, on this 1998 occasion, the weather was appalling with a gale-force wind and pouring rain, while the fourteen trams assembled on the Pleasure Beach outer loop. It was true that the official party left Crossbench-car 2 to a few delegates from the National Tramway Museum, while newly restored Crossbench 619 remained totally empty. With the planning of such a situation, saloon-cars 40 and 167 had been reserved for the official party, which were thus fully occupied! However the loyal enthusiasts took their places on the open cars such as Marton 31, Boat 600, and Princess Alice 706, while others sheltered on restored Balloon 700 and Coronation 660 - which were full! Of the conventional cars - Twin-car 674-684, Brush 631, and Jubilee 762 - were partially empty, but the final tram - rebuilt-Balloon 707 - was filled as a novelty.

The journey to Fleetwood was unfortunately not watched by any crowds, since people were sheltering in their cars, hotels, shop-fronts and tram shelters. When the procession arrived at Fleetwood led by Crossbench-car 2, I watched it turn into Bold Street and unload. The official party entered the North Euston Hotel for lunch, and many others went to see the Festival of Model Tramways at the Promenade Sports Centre. The open cars were sent back to the depot, and I watched this strange sight of unusually empty trams parading along North Albert Street. However Box 40 and Pantograph 167 were stored on the Ferry siding, ready to transport the official party back to Blackpool when the

to Fleetwood

Showing destination "FLEETWOOD" 167, 31, 600 of the Grand Cavalcade arrive here in the pouring rain.
Author

proceedings were finished. In the Ballroom of the North Euston Hotel the gathering was interesting, seeing delegates from the new tramway systems of Manchester, Sheffield, Birmingham and Croydon. In his speech, Managing Director Tony Depledge reflected on the success of this famous light-rail tramway for a hundred years, and as the only survivor in Britain became an example to the new Tramway generation! However, he did regret that the weather had haunted the proceedings that day. When 40 & 167 returned to Blackpool full of guests, their sight with trolley-ropes billowing behind, provided a picturesque finale to the day!

With driver Alan Williams, 31 turns into Bold Street with its anorak dressed passengers!
James Millington

67

Fortunately during the week, between the stormy Sunday of the Centenary Cavalcade and Fleetwood Tram Sunday, the weather was better and so provided a good scene for the appearance of the vintage trams on several occasions. On Monday evening, Pantograph 167 made a solo journey from the depot to Fleetwood, to give an excursion to the Fleetwood Tram Sunday Committee and the owners of the North Euston Hotel. As a native of this area, I stood at Rossall Lane tram stop and waited for 167. When it appeared round the corner towards the stop, it filled me with nostalgia. When I boarded it, I enjoyed the charm of the saloon, as I did as a conductor forty years ago! The ride to the Pleasure Beach for the guests was comfortable and spacious, and they were served with drinks to celebrate the occasion. Supper was taken on board 167, while it was standing on the outer loop there. Once the party returned to the North Euston Hotel, I stayed on 167 and travelled back to Rossall - as a local resident. Having got off, I stood and watched the Pantograph car disappear into the darkness, with its saloon lights gleaming and its trolley-rope swinging artistically behind. Undoubtedly it is part of the Blackpool & Fleetwood Tramroad history, and we look forward to seeing a restored Pantograph-car 174 one day!

Tuesday was notable for the use of distinctive Blackpool trams on the Fleetwood route, and it was delightful to see the once familiar Coronation car 660 picking up local passengers, in addition to the enthusiasts. Certainly, it always attracts the attention of the public, who are glad to ride upon it, being spacious and having comfortable seats. In the evening I saw it stopping at Lindel Road tram stop, parallel to Centenary 646 going in the other direction, and the contrast proved that 660 was the better designed of the two! Also there appeared Marton open-top 31 and Box 40, which were unusual in being seen in the evening and thus were well-patronised. On the following day, there was a display of the works cars on the triangle in front of the depot, including Engineering car 754, Grinder 752 with cable-reel trailer, Permanent-Way 259 and rail-trailer 260. The unique re-created Vanguard 619 - wrongly fitted with a pantograph - was offering rides along Blundell Street.

Historic-service - Vanguard 619 in Bold Street. **James Millington**   *& The familiar sight of Coronation car 660 at Rossall Lane.* **Author**

A historic scene of the visiting cars 2 & 167, together with Box 40, at the familiar Ferry terminus. They show the development of the fleet over the first thirty years.
Author

The final scene at Lytham Road - with 2, 40 & 167 - returning to the depot after their last tour together here. **Graham Weaver**

Following this, on Thursday there was a memorable tour of the system, using Crossbench-car 2, Box 40 and Pantograph 167. Collecting their passengers at the Tower, the three vintage trams travelled to Little Bispham loop where they turned for Norbreck, and reversed here for Fleetwood. Here there was a short shuttle journey to Ash Street, from whence they returned to the Ferry and posed together on the siding. Ironically, 167 stood alongside 2, showing a traditional NORTH STATION BLACKPOOL on its front indicator, but this was changed to RESERVED, in order to avoid confusing the normal passengers! In the sunshine, it made the three cars distinctive amongst all the ordinary service trams, and reminded me of 1960 when Crossbench-car 2 was used on the PROMENADE CIRCULAR, while 40 was always used as a Fleetwood Special on Market Days, although 167 was at that time a Works-car. On this occasion forty years later, I watched these three vintage trams return to Blackpool, travel along Central Promenade and turn into Lytham Road on their way back to the depot. Unfortunately, this was a final appearance here of Crossbench-car 2, having been restricted to private-hire usage and kept away from the public of a seaside resort!

The Final Weekend with Tram Sunday

Saturday 18th July - the last weekend of the Centenary - saw an F.T.S. final tram tour on Marton 31 and Pantograph 167, with the sunshine brightening the sight of the two cars, in contrasting colours! Visiting Fleetwood Ferry, Thornton Gate and Harrowside, the travellers enjoyed this rare experience, although some may recall a 1985 tour of 167 and Standard 40 together. Following this, Tram Sunday dawned with poor weather again, but there was quite a crowd at Fisherman's Walk to meet the tram procession at 11-30 a.m.. On this occasion it was led by Pantograph 167 and followed by Marton 31, Box 40, Vanguard 619, the new-looking 707 and Bolton 66. Once the Wyre Mayor had declared it open, Fred Dibnah led the procession with his traction-engine, followed by bands and dancers, with the trams. Travelling on 167 was a distinguished company - including Joan Hubble M.P. - who were dressed in Edwardian vintage costume. The large crowd in the rain waved to the official passengers enjoying the luxury of this saloon, and fortunately the weather improved at the mid-day. During the afternoon the trams travelled in pairs through the crowds, and were filled with passengers who enjoyed the advantage view of many historic buses, traction engines and cars. At 5 p.m. the vintage trams returned to Blackpool, having added greatly to a splendid Transport Festival - a fine tradition since 1985! This was the finale of the Centenary celebrations, which had been all too brief, but highly successful. In Fleetwood, there was much regret that Crossbench-car 2 had not been allowed to come, even though the Tram Sunday Committee had contributed towards the expense of its presence here!

A view of 167 reversing at Norbreck, from a vantage position on 31 during the final tour. **James Millington**

The sight of two red and white open-toppers, as 31 leaves the depot and Stockport 5. **Author**

A Nostalgic Look at the Vintage Trams

The final Illuminations weekend in 1998 enabled the F.T.S. to use Marton 31 and Brush-car 636 together for the last time, in this evening view at the Ferry.
Terry Daniel

A final scene in 2000, with 40 seen in the snow at Harrowside, during its annual tour for Friends of 40.
Steve Palmer

Back Cover:

Stockport 5 on tour at the Fleetwood Ferry siding 1998
R.P. Fergusson

Nostalgic sight of Standard 160 at Talbot Square 1962
Steve Palmer

A dramatic view of Crossbench 2 with the Tower 1998
Steve Palmer

Pantograph 167 & Marton 31 at Fleetwood Ferry 1998
Graham Weaver

Strolling people and parked vintage buses, provide an unusual scene for Marton 31 on Tram Sunday.
Terry Daniel

14th
Tram Sunday

A decorous pace amongst the wandering public enables individuals to examine detail on the side of 167, and ensure safety on Tram Sunday!
Terry Daniel